Live a Better Life

Using the science of behavior to drive
personal and social change

3344 Peachtree Road NE, Suite 1050
Atlanta, GA 30326

Live a Better Life

*Using the science of behavior to drive
personal and social change*

Aubrey C. Daniels, Ph.D. and A. Darnell Lattal, Ph.D.

© 2020 Aubrey Daniels International, Inc.

Performance Management Publications
a division of Aubrey Daniels International
3344 Peachtree Road NE, Suite 1050
Atlanta, GA 30326

Original cover design by Mark Robinson, Sr.

Printed in the United States of America

ISBN-10: 0-937100-29-3
ISBN-13: 978-0-937100-29-5

Praise for *Live a Better Life*

Live a Better Life offers readers a path with which to authentically better their lives by using the science of human behavior. Daniels and Lattal are known experts in the field with decades of successful applications of the science in settings ranging from oil fields to boardrooms, from homes to classrooms. But, as Daniels would acknowledge, of course their applications have been successful— it's science, after all! Together, they describe the science and strategies to proactively arrange the conditions necessary to thrive. Readers of all ages will come away with not only an understanding of why people do the things they do, but with tools that can be used to help themselves and others improve the human condition.

— Mary Sawyer, Ph.D., BCBA-D
Co-Owner & Director, Fit Learning Atlanta

Daniels and Lattal describe with great clarity how to change behavior as a way to unleash its untapped potential in shaping a better world.

—Robert Feldman, Ph.D., Professor of Psychological and Brain Sciences Deputy Chancellor, the University of Massachusetts, Amherst Author of *Understanding Psychology, Development Across the Life Span,* & *P.O.W.E.R. Learning: Strategies for Success in College & Life*

I have known Aubrey and Aubrey Daniels International for over twenty years and used his methods in creating easy ways to help business leaders understand the behavior of their workforce and themselves. This book offers a clear decision-making process for identifying what is helping or hindering positive outcomes. It is a brilliant tool for analyzing the situations that surround our behavior and arrange positive conditions for success. I find that using it to solve business problems is of great value, but using it within my family, I saw for perhaps the first time my own behavior much more clearly in terms of what I was doing that was helpful or not. I better understood me but also better understood my child. The positive solutions were so easy to apply. I now see all situations having to do with human behavior through this incredible approach and the power to leave us all much better off.

—Verne Harnish, Founder, ScaleUpU, Founder, EO, and author of *Scaling Up (Rockefeller Habits 2.0)*

Praise for *Live a Better Life*

Two experts in performance management explain how to bring about behavior change in a direct and understandable style. With handy tips like Positive-Immediate-Certain consequences and pinpointing for precision, average people as well as management will find *Live a Better Life* useful and eye-opening. I particularly liked the coverage of 'personality' as flexible—so often overlooked. Correspondingly, as the authors note, understanding behavior means avoiding the everyday labeling that can be so limiting and damaging.

—Susan Schneider, Ph.D.,
author of *The Science of Consequences*

By clarifying key principles from behavior science, and debunking commonly held beliefs about how our behavior "works," the authors provide a powerful strategy for anyone who will take the time to consider it: deliver positive, immediate, and certain consequences for the behavior we value. By applying this strategy, and the science behind it, we can magnify our positive impact on the world, one person at a time. Extended beyond our individual orbit of influence to the systems that educate our children and provide services to society, we can, indeed, bring true wisdom to human affairs, and help achieve outcomes to make a difference with our lives.

—Carl Binder, Ph.D., Co-founder,
The Performance Thinking Network;
President, The Fluency Project, Inc.

The authors, noted experts in the field of human performance management and behavior change, have written an extraordinarily helpful book on how to make decisions not only when life throws you a curve ball, but how to make good choices, big and small, throughout the day. This book is a must read for anyone teaching, managing, working with, or living with others—rarely are we presented with such a comprehensible, logical, and successful way of making change not only transparent, but achievable.

—Janet S. Twyman, Ph.D., BCBA, LBA, Director of
Innovation and Technology, Center on Innovations in Learning

Contents

Acknowledgements

We wish to thank the many people who are working to expand our own understanding of the science of behavior to improve individual success in accomplishing positive outcomes at home, in school, at work, and in the larger community. Additionally we have been influenced by the actions of many whose work and stories are recorded in this book. While we do not identify them in every case, almost all the case studies are from our work as clinicians or consultants. We owe our clients a special debt of gratitude for bringing these principles to life and allowing us to learn, while helping them make their lives better. They have definitely enriched ours.

Several people directly helped us by reviewing and advising us on various iterations of this book. They include Julie Terling, Cindy Ashworth, Laura-Lee Glass, Janet Lund, Francisco Gomez, Ken Wagner, Candi Sue Cross, Mary Sawyer and Verne Harnish. We thank them. Andy Lattal provided an in-depth analysis of the science behind the concepts and terms we used. We owe him a debt of gratitude for the care he took to help us. Gail Snyder read multiple versions of the book, providing detailed edits as it evolved and for that endurance and skill we are always grateful. Any failure to take the good advice offered from all belongs solely to us.

We are both indebted to one another as colleagues and friends who said a while ago, knowing not of what we spoke, "Lets write a book together." We share a worldview about behavior and how it can shape a better future. We desperately want to share it with others.

This journey gave us at least two more books' worth of writing that made the discard pile, but in the end, we came to appreciate, more fully, why we wanted to write this book together and how we added to one another's point of view. Neither of us could have written this book without the other and our personal worlds are better for this collaboration. We hope this book makes your world a better place as well.

We dedicate this book to our grandchildren—Julia Grace, Calista, Brendan, Ava, Alex, Ella, Nicholas, Elijah, Liam, and Aubrey. May they find that their lives are full of positive reinforcement and that the choices they make lead to a joyful and meaningful life for each of them, for others around them, and for the larger world.

—Aubrey C. Daniels & Darnell Lattal

Introduction

Since the first humans began interacting, there have always been those who wanted to influence others about the choices made in their personal and daily lives—how to lead, how to raise children, what to believe, and how best to live. The solutions offered about how to achieve these objectives all too often failed to deliver expected results.

Today, advice givers abound. They offer good or bad counsel about how to manage our behavior and are equipped with the amazing opportunity to distribute their words through books, the Internet, and on social media. On a given day in the summer of 2019, Amazon listed 146,025 books on leadership, 17,020 on childrearing, and 53,987 about living a good life.

Wise decision-making in the Information Age is complicated. People searching for answers may accept advice that confirms their biases without validating the veracity of that information. John P. Ioannidis, Professor of Medicine and Health Research at Stanford University, examined medical studies in reputable journals and found that as much as 90 percent of the published medical information relied upon by doctors, is flawed.[1] Similarly there is a lot of advice out there about what to believe, how to live a good life, and how to make personal changes to reach your potential. However, this advice may be based on theory or desire and not on a clearly examined process.

Underlying all of that advice about our behavior is the *science* of behavior (Behavior Analysis) that provides principles to help us look objectively at how to maintain, suppress, or accelerate behavior. The principles in this book come from that particular methodology, which has been replicated thousands of times through scholarly research. These principles provide reliable and valid results as to how people learn and under what conditions. There is a robust, science-based technology available to explore the ways in which behavior responds to the environment. The principles in this book are a surefire way to help you make thoughtful choices in changing the way your world works.

While technology is changing fast in ways that make it easier to do almost anything (think driverless cars and job automation), the way we learn, and how habits are acquired and strengthened, has not changed in thousands of years. It is time to understand these principles of learning: *everyone* needs these skills.

In 1964, songwriter, performer, and Nobel Laureate Bob Dylan wrote, *The Times They Are A-Changin'*, but he most likely did not anticipate the rate of change in our world today, and the unrelenting challenge of changing our behavior just to keep up. There is an urgent need for knowledge about how to change, but also to do so in a way that benefits individuals and society. Most people have good and honorable intentions, but these intentions matter little if their actions do not achieve the desired result. This book will provide you with the methods to do just that. As you read, you will learn the essential principles of how to change behavior while making this a better world for you and others.

If there had been public newspapers and a literate population to read them in the early days of ancient Rome, the headlines would probably not be distinguishable from those in the newspapers today. Stealing, bullying, and cheating were rampant. Water, air, waste pollution, and even traffic congestion, made everyday living difficult. People were seen as bad or good by nature. Property rights and personal security could never be taken for granted. Going to war was a common method of solving disputes.

Few would say that substantial progress has been made in the last 2,000 years. These problems not only still exist, but they consume enormous resources and funds, not to mention the human suffering they cause. People are still seen as having either great potential or very little, based not on capability but on bias about that potential. These problems all boil down to human behavior and how environmental conditions are used to either advance or limit what people can accomplish.

We begin with a true story to illustrate how biases about one's ability to learn, and a lack of scientific knowledge about behavior, limit the potential of others. We hope that by the end of this book you are as optimistic as we are about how this robust science of human behavior can influence our world for the better.

Part I

Behavior: Driving Personal and Social Change

1

Life's a Picnic

The Past is Not Prologue

We begin with a story of Junior Hall, a patient at the Georgia Regional Hospital of Atlanta (GRHA), an inpatient mental-health facility.

The GRHA was one of several regional mental-health facilities built in the 1960s to relieve the severe overcrowding at the Central State Hospital (claimed to be the largest in the world), which had about twice as many patients as it was built to house. The strategy of the state mental health department was to move patients closer to their relatives.

GRHA opened in 1968 and was quickly at capacity, housing 500 patients, many of whom had been hospitalized for decades. Because of the overcrowding, they received very little treatment. Each hospital served a wide range of issues from drug and alcohol abuse to developmental disabilities.

The superintendent at the facility was determined to make a difference in patient treatment and outcomes, and instituted a system-wide behavioral technology program as an efficient way to develop behaviors needed when patients were released and returned to their families and communities.

Although many had been hospitalized for most of their lives, patients suddenly began to do extraordinary things. Everyday accomplishments were described as mini-miracles through the systematic application of this science-based technology. Patients who were thought to be chronically unmotivated were discharged within weeks, not years. Although the percentage of statewide recidivism was over 70 percent, at GRHA it was 9 percent in the first year and 11 percent in the second.

Junior Hall was a teenager who was transferred from Central State Hospital where he had resided since shortly after birth. He was transferred to the Developmental Disabilities Unit of GRHA. Not only did the patients in this unit not walk, but many did not respond to their names, did not speak, feed, or dress themselves. Most were not toilet-trained.

Jordi Waggoner, a clinician on the psychology staff, immediately began a behavioral program with the attendants and nurses to teach the residents self-help skills (responding to their names, toileting, walking and feeding themselves). As a result of her work and skill, and with the help of the unit staff, 51 out of 60 residents were quickly taught these basic skills. Even so, because of their severe physical limitations, nine residents, including Junior, were assumed incapable of learning.

For example, according to his chart, Junior suffered from severe cerebral palsy and his IQ was estimated to be below 20. He had two movements of his body. He could move his head from side to side and had slight movement of his right wrist. Junior's cerebral palsy had crippled him to the point that he spent his days in a crib in the fetal position. He could not speak. Sometimes his crib would be moved so that he could watch television, not because the staff necessarily thought he would get anything from it, but because it seemed like the humane thing to do.

In addition to working with the staff to teach self-help skills, Jordi would also help feed the residents who were too physically handicapped to feed themselves. During her time spent with Junior, Jordi quickly became convinced that he had more capabilities than an IQ of less than 20 would predict. She approached her supervisor and asked if she could spend time working with Junior. When he asked her what she would like to do, she said, "Teach him to read." The supervisor, while very skeptical, told her that if she had the time it was okay with him.

The result was that over the course of several months, Jordi taught Junior to read! During her initial work with him he had mastered about 150 words. He could read simple books to himself and then answer multiple-choice questions by moving his wrist with a pointer firmly placed between his fingers, to indicate the correct choice. That summer Jordi assigned an intern from a local university to continue the work. The student was able to increase Junior's vocabulary by another 100 words. At this point employees on the unit began to speculate about just how smart Junior really was. Everyone who knew him was convinced that he was now functioning at only a very small part of his intellectual potential.

Trapped for almost 20 years by physical limitations and the perception that he couldn't learn, it was fortunate that Junior had Jordi to teach him. Wouldn't it be wonderful if all of our children could have a Jordi in their lives to *see* their behavioral potential and arrange positive conditions so that they too, might thrive? Her skill in helping Junior enter into a completely new world of possibilities came from what this science of behavior teaches us about the almost unlimited potential of everyone.

Why Write This Book?

Through decades of successful applications in homes, schools, and national and international work settings, we have seen firsthand how the laws of behavior have changed the world for the better. There are four intersecting reasons why we felt compelled to write this book.

1. To describe a science-based method for addressing human behavior that produces measurable, lasting, and scalable outcomes, based on factual understanding of causation. A comprehensive understanding of the science of behavior helps predict patterns of behavior and how conditions may affect future actions. We believe the more that everyone understands these universal principles, the more we all benefit.

2. To provide you with behavior-based decision tools that offer pragmatic ways to address daily problems and possibilities. The world needs clear methods to arrange conditions for positive behavior change, regardless of culture or histories of learning.

3. To increase awareness of how essential values are promoted, sustained, and transferred by what each of us says and does (behavior). Consider for example the *butterfly effect*, where a very small change in initial conditions can create an unexpected large effect later on. How people behave can have tsunami-like effects on others close by and far away.

4. To deliver science-based ideas that contribute to your understanding about what can affect individual and group change, and to inspire you to rethink how to address society's most critical human issues. Positive solutions to humankind's enduring problems are needed now.

This first chapter introduces you to an analysis of what influences behavior in positive or negative directions, even in the most complex or difficult patterns of behavior. This analytical tool is called the PIC/NIC Analysis®. By the end of this chapter, you will have a better understanding of why people behave as they do, even when their behavior initially appears illogical and strange to you. It will help you see clearly how the biases and assumptions that people bring to their environment can have a dramatic influence on their behavior. When you understand the science of behavior as Jordi did, feelings of blame or pity are replaced with possibilities and opportunities.

Changing Our Habits

Why is it so difficult for us to change our bad habits? Why can't we stay on a diet? Why can't we keep our New Year's resolutions? Why is it so challenging to maintain an exercise routine? You may ask yourself, "Why did I do that?" or "Why am I eating this dessert when I'm trying to lose weight?" or "Why do people smoke when they know that it could kill them?" or, "Why do parents abuse their children?" Why *do* people do things that seem self-destructive to their long-term self-interest? Why do people, as well as nations, perform destructive acts that harm entire communities or even the world?

In each instance that you ask, "Why do people do that?" or even "Why do I do that?" the PIC/NIC Analysis® shows you why and indicates how to arrange the environment to favor the behavior you want from yourself and others.[2] The PIC/NIC Analysis® is a user-friendly assessment of the conditions that govern the occurrence of behavior. Aubrey Daniels developed this tool from basic behavioral research of the environmental conditions that promote or impede desired change. Most importantly, it helps explain how various types of consequences and their timing accelerate or reduce the likelihood of planned or unplanned outcomes.

The PIC/NIC Analysis® is a way of analyzing the consequences of behavior to discover patterns that increase or decrease specific ways of responding in particular circumstances. It helps us understand the thorny problem of habits and how to address them. It is an effective way to move away from blaming people for their actions or inactions toward more objectively observing what people are doing. This science-based analysis clarifies how to arrange conditions so that new, more positive behaviors occur, without once having to find fault in the performer!

The science of behavior (a.k.a. behavior analysis) has demonstrated millions of times that the *consequences of behavior are the most important element in determining whether a behavior occurs*. What makes behavior more or less likely in the presence of various consequences is based on three critical elements—type, timing and predictability. These three elements influence the likelihood of behavioral change as the result of consequences. All three are important.

Classification of Consequences	
Type	**Positive** (something the performer wants)
	Negative (something the performer doesn't want)
Timing	**Immediate** (while the behavior is occurring)
	Future (any delay of more than a few seconds)
Probability	**Certain** (always follow the behavior)
	Uncertain (may or may not follow the behavior)

- Is the consequence positive or negative (P/N) to the person receiving it?
- Does it occur immediately after the behavior or in the future (I/F)?
- Is it most likely certain or uncertain that the particular consequence will occur (C/U)?

The table on the previous page provides the classification system for the many patterns that make it more or less likely that behavior will occur in particular circumstances.

What's In the Basket?

Throughout this book, we will provide information that helps you identify positive, immediate, and certain consequences (PICs) and understand their effects on behavior. You will then be able to arrange conditions that produce PICs to bring about desired changes in your life and the lives of others, ideally increasing success and personal happiness.

The PIC/NIC Analysis® applies to all questions of how the environment produces behavior that benefits or impedes the functioning of individuals and groups. As stated earlier, we all ask why people don't follow the rules that were meant to make everyone's lives better; questions like, "Why don't people obey traffic laws?" or "Why do able-bodied people park in spaces reserved for the handicapped?" or "Why do people litter or text while driving?" or "Why do people work in hazardous conditions without wearing their protective gear?" *Why, why, why?*

Most of us want to do things for our own good and express the desire to do things for the good of others (sometimes by the same actions). We can't always identify what doing good for others means. Sometimes even our good intentions to change our own behavior (New Year's resolutions, for example) end up with us quickly reverting to our old, ineffective, but often predictable patterns of behavior. One reason this happens is that many people believe having the desire or intention to change is enough, and consequently they fail to arrange what is needed to support new behavior.

When doing a PIC/NIC Analysis®, people find that the behavior(s) they want to increase for themselves or others often produce very few PICs, while the behavior they genuinely don't want to repeat continues and is actually strengthened because the undesired behavior continues producing its own PICs. Additionally, wanting to increase better personal habits or to learn a new skill often produces many NICs (negative, immediate, certain consequences), at least in the beginning.

Learning to do anything new is usually slower and more difficult when compared to old ways or habits, and often in the beginning produces many more errors. In other words, to make change easier, the behavior we want to increase needs to produce positive, immediate and certain consequences (PICs) to sustain our efforts. The behavior we want to eliminate needs to produce negative, immediate, and certain consequences (NICs) to help us stop behaving according to the old patterns that do not work for us.

Even when we are very excited about doing better, the *positive* consequences we focus on for the change are usually *future* and *uncertain* (PFU). Think about a New Year's resolution to lose weight: Food not on your diet tastes good immediately (PIC) although abstaining and exercising (NICs) will produce the desired result at some point in the distant future. Your clothes fit better and you look and feel better… someday (PFUs). The consequences of keeping that New Year's resolution are *exactly* the opposite of what we need.

By arranging consequences to favor productive, safe, and healthy patterns, or other valuable behaviors, it is easy to see from the PIC/NIC Analysis® why plans all too often have failed in the past and how we can develop plans in the future that increase the chances of success. Science tells us that most people rarely plan any PICs for the behaviors that result in attaining the goal. More often than not, they count on the attainment of the desired goal itself to provide the motivating consequences for developing the new habit. Sorry, but those new habits will happen rarely by relying on such a future, uncertain consequence to motivate daily activity. There are many things that affect how we respond to consequences, but immediate, positive and certain consequences increase behavior, as shown below.

The Relative Effects of Consequences

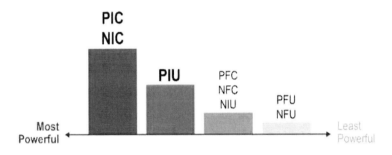

We all do what we do because consequences operate on the behavior of each of us in the same way, regardless of our unique circumstances. Consequences increase or decrease the likelihood of behavior. Because we learn from our environment, our experiences create consequences that shape our behavior, whether we are aware of that or not. Nature guarantees that no two people are the same because no two people, not even twins, have the exact same experiences. The *consequences* of our behavior provide the key to changing behavior. Even though each of us is different and our histories of learning are unique, our experiences—whatever they might be, impact and determine the way we respond in the present. We are all alike in this very basic way.

"The Devil Made Me Do It!"

Unfortunately, we attribute cause to many factors other than consequences in the environment. A well-known justification for why people do the wrong thing is that something inside their heads made them do the wrong thing. Flip Wilson was a famous, wildly popular TV comedian in the 70s whose character "Geraldine" justified her outrageous behavior by blaming the devil. As the comedian would often say, "The devil made me do it!" The devil says, "Have your pleasure now [PIC] and gamble that nothing bad will happen to you later [NFU]."

While it is easy to blame the devil (even though that is not what Geraldine really believed), the problem is that many people do attribute their actions and those of others to forces beyond their control. Why else would people behave so irrationally or unconventionally? The PIC/NIC Analysis® can help you figure that out, with no need for dark demons, bad character, uncontrollable feelings, or any other internal state to explain what is maintaining actions that need to change.

Good conscience, values, persistence, personal character, and even patterns of behavior that we call evil have their origins in a series of external PICs and NICs for doing either the right or wrong thing because of the social and natural "reinforcers" that maintain these actions.

Parents, Welcome to the Picnic!

For parents, having insight into the true causes of our children's behavior can be most helpful in changing behavior when children do things that they know are wrong, but do them anyway. Knowing about causation helps us to stay away from labeling children as "bad by nature" or "driven by terrible temperament," or any of the other ways we tend to dismiss bad behavior patterns by blaming an unseen force beyond the child's control. Parents want children to do the right thing for many reasons, not the least of which is because they know that beyond the thrill of the moment (positive, immediate, certain—PIC), doing the right thing will pay off over the long haul (positive, future, uncertain—PFU).

To help our children work hard for recognition or satisfaction in the future we must use many positive, immediate, and certain consequences (PICs) for behaviors along the way. What if parents frequently delivered PICs for behaviors that are consistent with the values they want to teach the child? You may remember doing those things your parents believed to be right, like shaking hands firmly with grownups, maintaining eye contact, saying "thank you" and talking to guests about your school activities. Even though your parents constantly reminded you to do those behaviors, you most likely did not see any immediate benefit for doing so (only NICs) unless you also understood that if you did these things you might be allowed to leave (PFU) and go do what you wanted to do (PICs).

But think about the times you did what you found to be fun. Participating in such activities repeatedly was easy (PICs). Children receive an endless stream of PICs for certain behaviors that they find enjoyable (such as playing video games, hide and seek, having sleepovers, talking on a cell phone, climbing trees, surfing the Web, riding bikes, or playing sports). Although many PICs exist for those behaviors, the PICs are often missing for the many behaviors that parents want the child to do instead. Parents who fail to reinforce the desired behavior in their children often excuse their own failure to do so by making statements like, "Having good manners is its own reward (PFU)." Parents have been taught, perhaps by their own parents, that no further action is needed to instill good manners.

Many parents have a difficult time separating the behavior of the child from the child. On occasion, when they can't understand their child's behavior, they revert to notions of DNA: "He is just like his father!" or "That side of the family has always acted like that." But more often than not, they blame the child for his behavior, as in, "What is wrong with you?" with an emphasis on *you*! The *Picnic* Parent learns that the sources of a child's behavior are in the child's environment and are determined by what happens when the child behaves or does not behave in a certain way. After all, Mark Twain's character Tom Sawyer wasn't a bad kid. He simply got more reinforcers from engaging in "free spirit" activities than from activities related to traditional rules and societal mores. For Tom, adventure certainly produced abundant PICs when traditional conduct only offered PFUs. Most of us in our childhood met that seemingly slightly dangerous and deviant ten-year-old boy, similar to "Cousin Bill." We may all have a few stories about trading the satisfaction of being a good child in our parents' eyes for the thrill of being, even if ever so briefly, just like deviant Cousin Bill. There was that special time climbing over the fence to steal Mr. Jones' green apples off his tree or skinny-dipping in the creek. When we were found out, it was always poor Cousin Bill's fault! He was often viewed as the troublemaker. The good cousins were viewed as behaving naively under his spell. This is another analogy for explaining why we do what we do: the charm, the fear, the power of the other person to "*make* us climb that apple tree."

Just like the rotten apple in the basket of fresh apples, Cousin Bill could have spoiled the whole bunch of cousins! When asked, "Why did you do that?" the cousins replied, "Bill MADE us do it!"

Such uninformed paradigms of causation (that a bad cousin or the devil is to blame) play a major role in inadvertently reinforcing many behaviors that create problems in families, workplaces, government, and society-at-large. Immediate consequences can be powerful even though the behavior is seemingly small (that first puff on a cigarette, the first sip of alcohol, taking drugs, and engaging in illegal behavior such as stealing or shoplifting). Consequences can appear to be single, individual events or they can be the accumulation of many small events that change behavior. The same process is involved in both.

Forbidden behaviors typically produce PICs for the performer, especially when the probability of the occurrence of NICs is very low, because the parent, teacher or colleague is not present. If appropriate behavior produced more PICs, negative behavior by the child (or the adult, for that matter) would be less likely.

"Consequences Made Me Do It"

When we act in a particular way, it isn't because of the devil or Cousin Bill. It is because we have a history of consequences that support those behaviors. The most certain thing we have in terms of a behavioral law, as gravity is a law of physics, is that *behavior is a function of its consequences*. Consequences that occur during or immediately after a behavior have the most impact on the behavior. Behavior that is positively reinforced immediately is most likely to be repeated, but positive reinforcement delivered in the future—later in the evening, the next day, or the next week—very often loses much of its impact on behavior.

We don't have a saying about the "good" child that parallels what we say about the "bad" child: "Cousin Bill is a bad playmate so stay away from him!" We never say, "Why don't you, my good child, play with Cousin Bill and help him be a better playmate?" For good reason. It is difficult for parents to compete with the tempting misadventures of childhood. It's surprising that more of us did not engage in even more devious behaviors as children. Yet as determined by Robert Eisenberger, a social psychologist at the University of Houston, we do know that the child who has an extensive history of PICs for appropriate behavior, and reinforcement for making choices that may cause a delay in receiving an immediate reward, is less likely to respond to peers and do the wrong thing.[3]

Learning to delay reinforcement allows us to develop greater persistence in working to complete a difficult task, even if we receive no recognition or reward from others around us. Finding plenty of positive, immediate and certain values in working hard over extended periods helps us to master new skills (piano, soccer, math, chess, art, science, etc.).

Teaching children how to make these kinds of choices, even when there are long delays before seeing results, is associated with wiser decision-making for the benefit of self and others throughout life. Learning to move away from highly reinforcing and immediate social pressure to persist on a difficult task is a particularly important skill for children (and adults) to learn. Persistence can be reinforced as a value in itself by parents and others, both in the initial stages of a task and as the child continues—with or without immediate or any visible success. Many behaviors learned as a child will remain with us for a lifetime.

One day while finding a place to sit for lunch while working at Xerox, I (Aubrey) noticed a man that I had seen before and asked to sit with him. While eating, the man related that he was retiring at the end of the month. I said that he must be happy about that. He responded, "Not really." "Why is that?" He continued. "My wife died a couple of years ago and I have found that now, although I have time to spend with my adult children, they don't have time to spend with me; they always seem to have other plans. However, my neighbor taught me a lesson, similar to what you are training us in here at Xerox. "As I watched my children drift further away from me, I continued to be puzzled by it. I was outside one afternoon when I noticed that one of my neighbors' grown children was cutting his grass and another was washing his car. That had always been the way it was but I had not really seen it before. When my wife was alive the children were always around. I just assumed that would continue. But now the behavior of my neighbor's children caught my eye.

I asked him, 'Why is it that I see your children at your house helping you do things when I can't get my children to come over?' He said, 'I don't know but I guess it started when they were just little things. I would say to my son, 'How about run get my paper?' When he would come back with it I would put a little dime in his hand. I would say to my daughter, 'Would you mind bringing me my slippers?' And when she returned, I put a little dime in her hand. They really took delight in those moments. I did too and they knew it.' Dang, Aubrey, I thought that was bribery and I never did anything like that with my kids. I was busy and my wife kept that side going."

Contrary to being bribery, his neighbor was, by the effective use of consequences, teaching his children that helping daddy had an immediate payoff and that daddy appreciated their effort. Long before they were adults, he no longer provided tangible rewards. The children continued to seek out ways to help their father, with clearly good feelings generated among the three of them when helping him, even into adulthood. Helping became a positive value in its own right, a basic goal that parents often have for their children. Some parents find that they, like the fellow at Xerox, might get help from their grown children only if they are provided tangible rewards for their efforts. This is one of the sadder consequences of failing to build a positive and mutually respectful relationship with our children, early in their lives.

Commanding Attention...Forever

When a child is interrupting adult conversations or turning cartwheels in the middle of the floor, parents often say, "Ignore him. He is just trying to get attention." This could imply that *grown-ups* don't do things for attention. Not so. Adults certainly do things, even outrageous things, for PICs. Our friends laugh at our jokes, listen to our concerns, like our new material possessions, and offer signs of approval (a smile, positive comments, advice), sometimes even when we do things wrong or do things that are not in our best interest.

The process of responding to social reinforcers starts when we are born and continues throughout our lives. PICs can generate good things or reinforce immature, annoying or dangerous habits, just as with the young cousins climbing over Mr. Jones' fence to pick an apple off his tree. Much more troubling behaviors are maintained by the same PICs whether during childhood or as adults.

Depending on the experiences people have, they will respond differently to the same situation. The person whose parents intervened mostly to correct misbehavior and used punishment excessively is more likely as an adult to respond similarly in his interactions with others, as compared to a person whose parents used positive reinforcement wisely. A person whose parents made many promises and delivered few may initially have a different reaction to a supervisor's promises about positive outcomes for work completed, than one whose parents consistently delivered on their promises. However, we cannot judge whether or not a child raised in an abusive home will be abusive, or one raised in a positive home will be positive in outlook and actions. What parents do and say can have a profound influence on us as we grow into adulthood, but other sources of influence start from the time we begin to interact with others outside our family. The influences on behavior are everywhere and often even the most optimistic and positive people we meet in life have had a difficult time growing up. When we look at the circumstances of their lives, we may be amazed at how they survived, much less became positive and productive.

The answer lies in the fact that neighbors, relatives, friends, teachers, and coaches may be more likely to be pleased with small improvements than family or even siblings. Many individuals report being alone a lot as children but finding PICs in the environment: hiking and fishing, reading books full of adventure, mastering a skill like throwing balls into a hoop, taking care of a pet, or other events that shape both productive and joyful activity. They often describe the growth of independence and self-confidence when they finally get away from excessively demanding and abusive situations.

We are continually experiencing PICs, NICs, PFUs, etc. during our lifetimes, and these experiences form our character which, to a rather large extent, determines what we say and do.

2

We Are Not Captive to Our Histories (*the picnic continued*)

Consistency between what is said and done is the behavioral definition of *trust*, which helps us predict how the world will treat us. If bad things are promised and then delivered, we may learn to expect such consequences in many settings. In a textile mill we worked in many years ago, employees rejected money (silver dollars) offered on the manufacturing floor as a bonus for good work because in the past such events had always been followed by a negative experience, such as being asked to work overtime on weekends or to perform undesirable tasks.

If the everyday experience of children is consistently inviting, warm, and friendly, they learn from those experiences. When the environment is negative, hostile, and otherwise aversive, children learn to respond to those experiences in a very different way.

When we have difficulty navigating through school or other settings, those consequences also shape us. Still, while behavior is predictable in that sense, it is also highly malleable, and never static, as we continue to learn from observing what happens. It is amazing the influence a teacher, neighbor, or relative can have on a child when commenting positively on his or her early attempts at drawing, telling stories, or singing. When adults are asked who had the most influence on their career, they are as likely to name a teacher or relative, as they are to name a parent. A few deliberately provided PICs can open up a world of otherwise unknown possibilities. The predictability of PICs delivered by our teachers for doing good work and other behaviors that please them increases the likelihood of our doing more. Children learn quickly.

Small positive changes in how others respond offer great opportunities for creating passion around the most unexpected events and activities, turning a disinterested student into a thoroughly informed person about the weather, frogs, math, dance or a million other things. A positive and specific comment about a drawing can open up the world of art and so on. Even more importantly, having teachers, relatives or friends provide positive comments or show interest in a child's ideas or activities, especially when the child does not get that at home, can do more than increase a skill. It can reassure the child, sometimes for the first time, of a personal capability to achieve something meaningful.

Unique histories produce unique individuals. The way our parents and other important figures treated us has a significant effect on our behavior as adults, particularly if those behaviors continue to produce results we want beyond childhood. Note, though, that contemporary experiences continue to change our histories of reinforcement and alter what we say and do in significant ways. Thus, we have the opportunity to change our reinforcement history many times every day. Change is not only possible; it is inevitable. The only question is whether the habits we make now will serve us well in the future.

Even though our histories of learning are different, people are alike in fundamental ways because we share the same consequences for much of our behavior in society. These rules of conduct shape the vast majority of us to do what is expected. We stop at stop signs when driving, look both ways before walking across the street, shake hands, smile, and greet most people with friendliness.

Because even the smallest environmental differences between any two humans can make a huge difference in how they respond to the world-at-large, these differences emphasize how the environment promotes change. They may be so small that they are difficult to observe, but the small PICs and NICs we receive for our behavior throughout our lives have a huge influence on what we become: musician, homemaker, teacher, truck driver, lift operator, scientist, criminal, opera or country music lover, or both.

Although consequences can be used in many ways to influence behavior, learning how to use the power of positive reinforcement effectively as a primary motivational tool will add immensely to your own life and to the lives of those you care about. Positive reinforcement (PICs) accelerates change at a rapid rate and quickly leads to mastery and fluency in learning and in creating strong habits.

We are all too familiar with punishment or negative strategies for influencing others. While such strategies may have been identified as working well in controlling a child's behavior, they produce numerous negative side effects. If you have ever experienced threat and/or fear, you understand how negative consequences work. Possible side effects include attempts to escape from fear, avoid threatening conditions, perform in minimally compliant ways, and even to seek revenge. We will have more to say about these strategies later.

This book focuses on accelerating the effects of consequences that increase *positive* behavior-change strategies. The science of behavior shows us that changing behavior through positive consequences is much more effective than using coercive, *negative* methods. Coercive methods are not only less effective than positive ones, but also usually have undesirable side effects such as blaming others, withdrawal, fear, and anger.

The PIC/NIC Analysis® in Greater Detail

To repeat, the PIC/NIC Analysis® helps move away from blaming and labeling. It moves toward observing, in more objective terms, what people are doing under current conditions and their reasons for doing so. It clarifies how to arrange conditions to support new patterns of behavior, without once blaming or labeling the performer.

Positive, immediate, and certain (PIC) consequences are most likely to sustain behavior but, as shown in the following table, the PIC/NIC Analysis® also includes other types of consequences:

> NIC (Negative, Immediate and Certain)
> PFC (Positive, Future and Certain)
> NFC (Negative, Future and Certain)
> PFU (Positive, Future and Uncertain)
> NFU (Negative, Future and Uncertain)

These tell you the *type* of consequence (P or N); the *timing* (I or F); and the *predictability* (C or U) of those consequences.

The following table provides a simple, yet clear way to understand how consequences impact behavior. In this example, a factory operator working on equipment is more likely to do things that may be dangerous, even though common sense might indicate that it would be foolish. Common sense in such situations is no guide because there are more PICs than NICs for acting in an unsafe manner in the workplace. Such PIC/NIC Analyses® are done in great detail to understand why certain desired or undesired behaviors occur. The PIC/NIC Analysis® can be used in any circumstance, whether at work, at home, or for self-change.

PIC/NIC Analysis® Operator Behavior
Behavior: Clearing a jam while machine is still running

Antecedents	Consequences	P/N	I/F	C/U
Schedule demands	Save time	P	I	C
Backlog while machine is down	No rewarm-up period	P	I	C
Boss wants higher productivity	Stay on schedule	P	I	C
Feedback graphs for machine uptime	Lose a finger	N	I	U

© 2019 Aubrey Daniels International, Inc.

While the PIC/NIC Analysis® is not a certain predictor of exactly how a person will respond, it allows a quick understanding as to why certain behaviors are likely to occur in a given circumstance. It provides a guide for what you may need to do if you are a supervisor, parent, or coach, to encourage safer, healthier, more productive practice, to complete a task, or to learn a new skill in the correct way.

Remember that a NIC is as effective in stopping a behavior as a PIC is in increasing one. Remember as well that a negative consequence that is immediate and uncertain (NIU) has considerably less power to stop a behavior than a negative consequence that is immediate and certain (NIC). Hitting your finger with a hammer does not stop you from using a hammer in the future, because after the first painful punishment, you are likely to be more careful in the future! Intermittent, positive consequences actually strengthen behavior, as in panning for gold in a mountain stream. Occasionally finding even the smallest of gold nuggets will keep you look-ing for quite a while. Intermittent, irregularly occurring rein-forcement is one of the ways that many tasks are sustained until a long-term task is accomplished.

Unfortunately, the forms of consequences commonly used to motivate behavior are the PFU and NFU. If you work hard, you will be successful (PFU). If you put in the extra effort, you might get a promotion (PFU). If you get caught doing things against the rules you might be fired (NFU). If you speed, you could get a speeding ticket (NFU). "If you do that, she might get angry!" (NFU). The list goes on and on. NFUs are not very effective. Think about crime: you may or may not get caught. Think about eating a healthy diet and exercising as a way of extending your life, or saving for the future. It's easy to procrastinate on behaviors that don't have an immediate payoff. It is much more fun to eat what we want when we want it (which is a PIC).

Knowing that PFUs and NFUs are not very effective, how do people sustain behavior over time when reinforcement is distant and uncertain (PFUs)? The sustaining elements are small reinforcers that people who understand the effectiveness of PICs experience in directing their actions toward purposeful objectives. One element we often asso-ciate with maturity is called *delay* of reinforcement. The inability to delay reinforcement is often called *impulsivity* and is generally considered a sign of immaturity. Most of us learned in childhood that many things cannot be hurried, even if we had very permissive or doting parents. Summer vacation, holidays, birthdays, and the end of the school year could not be hurried, so we learned to wait.

Everyone who has children, or has ever been one, knows the routine of taking children on a road trip. Before you get to the end of your block, voices from the back seat start asking, "Are we there yet?" While it may take many trips before they stop asking, they finally do because they learn that it does indeed take a certain amount of time to drive many miles to the beach or other fun destinations.

Most of us have learned that we can shorten delay for something we want by increasing our behavior, as in "When you finish your homework, you can go play." Or, in some situations, we learned that delay in getting something immediately results in a better or larger payoff later. "When I finish cutting the grass, I will go play golf." Or "You can spend your money for candy now or put it in the bank and buy that toy you want later." If you waited for something you wanted, you most likely did receive a larger or better payoff later, and you learned to trust that the environment was predictable. That is, that a promise made would actually pay off, if you did what was asked.

In the now-famous *Marshmallow Test*, developmental psychologist Walter Mischel studied what he called self-control[4] in children who managed to wait before taking something they wanted. The experimenter placed a marshmallow on a plate while saying that he had to leave the room briefly, but if the child did not eat the marshmallow until the experimenter returned, the child could then have two. If the child ate the marshmallow before he returned, the child would not receive the second one. In fact, some children ate the one marshmallow immediately. Others, however, showed a variety of behaviors that helped them wait without eating, such as turning away, humming, wiggling, talking to themselves, drumming fingers, petting the marshmallow, counting, or looking around the room.

The results demonstrated that children who behaved immediately in ways that kept them engaged in alternative behaviors to eating were most likely to succeed. The evidence suggests that those who waited had learned that doing what was asked, paid off. They demonstrated what is called *trust*. That is, they had learned that there is a direct relationship between what is promised to them and what actually happens. Following the rules can be expected to lead to good things.

Ten years later, and at intervals across their lives, the children who waited were measured on a variety of life tasks and academic achievement when compared to those who did not delay eating that first marshmallow. Those who waited were judged to be significantly more capable across many areas of development associated with a lifetime of success factors, including higher scores on college admission tests, financial success, and social and personal satisfaction.

The major differences in whether someone succeeds in delaying an immediate reward for something better later, lies in part in how they are taught. That is, there is a predictable relationship between what a child does and what happens to that child. To increase that sense of predictability it is very important to have parents, teachers and others in a child's life delivering on promises made for requested behavior. Such trust influences us our whole life long.

Persistence and other qualities generally valued by parents and society at large are all produced through the pattern of intermittent positive consequences that one experiences. This kind of early training helps us learn that our behavior will pay off down the road. This is how we learn persistence and that working hard is "its own reward." Many skills are required to play the piano, be good at soccer, compete in ballet, or write a book: all require persistence (practice and correction, again and again) and may be surrounded at first by a fair number of NICs. If used correctly, plenty of PICs are available to keep this pattern going.

If at first you don't succeed, try and try again, while seeking corrective feedback. You eventually experience the pleasure of doing things you did not know you could do at first. From such daily, persistent patterns come some of the world's greatest accomplishments. Helping children understand that persistence pays off will do them well throughout life. Lessons that were not taught early in life, like the benefits of persistence, certainly can be learned in later life, but there are distinct advantages to starting early.

The high pace at which humans are capable of learning and doing things that are reinforcing is captured by the Discretionary Effort Model©. Discretionary effort is often observed in the workplace when an individual or group accomplishes more than was required or expected while performing at rapid rates of skill acquisition or problem solving, to achieve desired outcomes. The Discretionary Effort Model visually demonstrates what happens to skill mastery when people are in conditions where there are high and steady rates of positive reinforcement.

Capturing Discretionary Effort

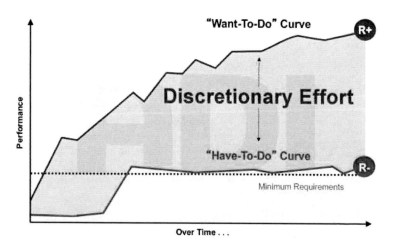

© 2019 Aubrey Daniels International, Inc. www.aubreydaniels.com/discretionary-effort

Those who master piano, golf, chess, Rubik's cubes, deep sea fishing, ice skating, cross-country skiing, crossword puzzles, math problems, German, mechanical problems, writing, and so on, establish life-long skills that come from repeating practice that takes on properties of positive reinforcement. "The more I practice, the better I get." Learning to strive toward as much "perfect" practice as possible in learning a difficult task leads to valuable lifelong habits of not only accomplishment but also of knowing how to learn. For example, it is not just practice while repeating errors over and over that will improve your golf swing. Rather, it is learning to make error-free gains through *deliberate* practice.

Although mastering a particular skill can take any number of hours of practice, it is not simply about hours. It is about *how* you practice. You may have heard it takes 10,000 hours to become an expert. Dr. Anders Ericsson, the expert on optimal performance gains to whom this trope is ascribed, never actually said that. Rather he wrote about practicing while trying to get better. Of course, to know that you are getting better you have to track performance. Thus, it is with deliberate practice leading to error-free learning where phenomenal gains in skill occur. To assume learning must be hard to be worthwhile is to misunderstand how much success accelerates in all kinds of learning (chemistry, physics, tennis, dance) when it is easy and fun. Deliver PICs, not NFU consequences, for efficient learning.

Procrastination is another pattern at the opposite end of persistence. Those who procrastinate are in an environment where PICs are only available for the non-desirable behaviors and at best only PFUs are available for the desirable ones. Almost everyone remembers turning in a term paper at the last minute and receiving an A on it. This actually strengthens the habit of procrastination because you got to do some things you wanted to do and still got a good grade on the paper that you procrastinated on. Playing a computer game instead or doing your homework or talking to friends in the workplace when you should be completing tasks are also familiar examples. In an environment where behavior competes for PICs over PFUs, the PICs win almost every time.

People procrastinate in situations where the primary consequences for doing a task quickly or on time are NFU. The quality of work suffers when the only consequence to the performer is completing the work. Procrastination is not a fault of character but of contingencies of reinforcement. As much as possible, create environments where high and steady states of positive reinforcement are generously available for the behaviors of working on a paper or project, and not just for when the work is finished.

All of us tend to sum up the patterns of behavior we observe, and at times are usually certain we understand why people do what they do based on how we interpret their behavior. We assume as well that we know how to help them improve. We are often wrong. The next chapters will help you define behavior more objectively, a necessary step before you can use your knowledge of these principles of behavior to effectively manage change in yourselves and others.

Reference: PIC/NIC Analysis® Combinations

PIC – Positive Immediate Certain consequence. Occurs immediately following a behavior. Is the most effective way to increase behavior. "Catch 'em in the act." Great way to build new behaviors to habit strength.

PIU – Positive Immediate Uncertain consequences. This would be described as "intermittent positive reinforcement." After a behavior is well established this approach can be effective in maintaining the behavior.

PFC – Positive Future Certain consequences. PFCs are essentially rewards. Because they are delayed and often not contingent on specific behaviors, their effect is reduced in relation to a PIC. However, well established behavior patterns are maintained often under such consequence management.

PFU – Positive Future Uncertain consequences. With PFUs the consequence has a low probability of happening. Winning the lottery is a good example. Even though winning is associated with a large payoff, a small percentage of the population sticks with it. However, many people will still engage in such unlikely behavior for such things as a possible bonus at the end of the year. They have come to believe based on their history that persistence often pays off even if uncertain.

NIC – Negative Immediate Certain consequences. Occurs immediately after a behavior. NICs are as effective in stopping a behavior as PICs are in increasing a behavior. Negative consequences that occur immediately are considerably more effective than those that are delayed. They are the most effective consequence for stopping undesired behavior and often involve active punishment (verbally and sometimes physically) or withdrawal of attention or other desired support. The by-products for those who use NICs are large and can last a lifetime. There are better ways to use consequences for the good of all.

NIU – Negative Immediate Uncertain consequences. Intermittent punishment is generally ineffective in stopping behavior. Having to increase the intensity or length of punishment is an indication that the consequence is ineffective. Most often this inconsistency leads to distrust and the assumption that nothing really will happen. When it does, it can often appear arbitrary and capricious to the person receiving a NIU in real time.

NFC – Negative Future Certain consequences. Delayed negative consequences are generally ineffective but their looming certainty suppresses ease of learning and increases a rather constant fear reaction. NFCs are commonly used in parenting as a threat of what will definitely happen as the child continues doing whatever it is the parents do not want; law breaking is another where jail definitely looms for certain acts but may not stop criminal behavior because it is also unlikely the person will be caught. This strategy is used in business where employees know that if they or their team fail to achieve a goal, they could easily be replaced or badly embarrassed for the failure—and that they *will* be. All of which is not desired. The threat is always there and it is real. While they are not as effective as PFCs, NFCs have a destructive quality to those who are under this condition, diminishing loyalty and trust.

3

From Labels and Assumptions to Words and Deeds

Although many people think they understand how behavior works, our experience is that they do not. They know enough to talk about relationships and how people act at a party, at work, or at home, but when it comes to changing unhealthy or unproductive behavior, people often lack the knowledge and skill to do so and seldom agree with family, friends and co-workers on how or what should be done. They even disagree about the meaning of the word *behavior*.

To explore the causes of behavior defined in the PIC/NIC Analysis®, it is important to know what behavior is and is not. Many people talk about behavior as private, belonging only to the individual, and thus not observable by others. Or they talk about behavior as being superficial and external. First defining behavior clearly and then becoming objective about what behavior is and is not are central to figuring out what is maintaining effective and not-so-effective behavior patterns. How we define behavior can enhance or distort our ability to pinpoint behavior change with the precision we need.

Behavior is what we say and do. The behavior in a PIC/NIC Analysis® is what is observable by others. Behavior can be public or private. Public behavior is any behavior that can be observed or verified by others at home or in a public place. Private behaviors are those sometimes richly entertaining private events that go on in our heads, where we may say to ourselves, "If only they knew what I was thinking!" while we smile politely through a boring talk about new performance-appraisal practices at work. Luckily, even with current technological advances, private thought is still private, knowable only to the individual.

Aubrey's Case Study: Start in the Present, Not in the Past

Regardless of what you saw in the movies, uncovering or reliving some repressed traumatic memory of the past is rarely needed to solve many behavior problems.

If you have agoraphobia, which is a fear of open spaces, there is no need for anyone to explore your sexual history, search for some childhood trauma, or discuss a relationship when you were abused, neglected, or otherwise treated poorly. In the case of the typical agoraphobic, friends and family are often impatient with small improvements and try to convince the patient that the environment is indeed safe. Agoraphobics have learned through many events to be afraid of open spaces (most often outdoors), and the job of the therapist is to teach them to be comfortable in those open spaces.

For example, one of my agoraphobic clients could not walk down the walkway in front of the office to the sidewalk by herself, a distance of about 20 feet. She would not do anything outside by herself. She had received electroshock treatment for 26 of her 52 years. Her 1960s-trained, psycho-analytic psychiatrist appraised her situation as, "Having a desire to return to the womb." In other words, he would say that inside her house she felt safe and secure and the outdoors represented physical and psychological harm.

In contrast, I described her difficulty as having learned to be afraid of the outdoors. Her task was to learn to feel comfortable and secure while alone outside. After teaching her relaxation techniques and setting very small goals, she literally overcame her phobia by walking an increasing number of steps each day until she was able to freely move around outside as needed. She was discharged from the inpatient hospital in less than six weeks.

Behaviors that had been tormenting her for most of her life were changed dramatically. She got a job, travelled internationally with her husband, and otherwise functioned without "phobic" behavior until her death 40 years later. By pinpointing her problem in terms of overt behavior rather than an internal conflict due to ill-defined trauma, the treatment, while warm and caring, was straightforward. Progress was easily measured and success clearly seen by others.

At the time, this treatment was considered radical and even called dangerous by staff psychiatrists, as it did not appear to deal with the speculated underlying issues of the patient. We did not need to probe into that part of her life, but that did not mean that their relationship was anything other than profound. The words she had used to describe her situation changed as her behavior began to change.

As she began to see the changes in her behavior, all kinds of new ways of acting and describing herself began to occur. She called me on my birthday every year for 40 years until her death, to update me on her accomplishments and to inquire about my family. If I had dealt first with the patient's "desire to return to the warmth and safety of the womb," how long do you think it would have taken me to rid her of this phobia?

Today, this behavioral treatment for phobias is a widely accepted treatment. If you are living with an agoraphobic, you may find this analysis too simple. However, for this person and numerous others subsequently treated, it changed their lives forever. We do not want to imply that all people who are afraid to go outside are in need of a simple plan of shaping (which we will introduce in Chapter 4); however, research shows clearly that the most effective solution is through the modification of conditions and consequences that sustain current patterns. Still, too many traditionally trained mental health professionals, while conceding that the cause of most problems is external, continue to insist that a lasting solution (symptom-free life) requires that the patient search for past events and memories to be reinterpreted with the professional to achieve the real cure.

It is true that there are people who are very disturbed who have verbal and behavioral patterns that are called psychotic or who would fit a diagnosis as described in the *Diagnostic and Statistical Manual of Mental Disorders, Fifth Edition* (DSM–5) requiring both medication and behavioral treatment (hearing voices, speaking incoherently, extreme aggression, murderous rages, seeing things that are not there, disabling depression, stress disorders, traumatic brain injury, drug and alcohol addictions, and so on).

Some of these problems include physical causes and require medical and in-patient treatment to protect them from doing harm to themselves and others or having others do harm to them. However, a bold experiment in the mid-1960s changed the way many think about mental illness.

One of the great lessons from early pioneers in the field of behavior analysis is just how much the environment controls actions, even those listed in DSM–5. In their book, *The Token Economy*, Drs. Nate Azrin and Ted Ayllon described one of the first applications of behavioral techniques in a special, behavior-based ward at Anna State Hospital[5]. Their ward was filled with people labeled schizophrenic, paranoid, manic-depressive, and so on.

A very unusual aspect of the study was that patients' psychotropic medications were stopped. Then, the focus of treatment was on reinforcing adaptive behavior by giving patients tokens they could exchange for valued personal items, each time they engaged in positive actions. Over time, old repetitive behaviors such as constant rocking, leaving social situations to sit in isolation, pacing back and forth, crying, or loud and inappropriate outbursts were replaced by more normal, socially appropriate patterns. While less physically incapacitated than Junior Hall was in the description at the start of this book, these patients responded as he did to the systematic applications of PICs and NICs to reinforce and sustain more independent and satisfying patterns of behavior.

In many cases, after only a few weeks, these patients dressed and groomed themselves, played cards, socialized, and walked around the grounds unescorted or with other patients. They also cleaned and maintained their rooms and worked in the small, token-economy store where patients exchanged tokens for candy and other small, personal items. Dr. Halmuth Schaefer of Patton State Hospital in California achieved similar results, documented in the film *Reinforcement Therapy*. Similar results were also achieved at Bryce State Hospital in Alabama where the psychology staff was awarded a hospital improvement grant to establish a token economy with 16- to 29-year-old schizophrenics. In these programs, it was not unusual for patients hospitalized for decades to be returned to their families and communities.

How these long-institutionalized individuals were shaped to interact normally after years of medication and constraints, without antipsychotic medications, is a story we do not want to be forgotten.

These methods freed so many from the debilitating limitations of ineffective behavior patterns and in their place taught effective and socially appropriate ones. These settings were among the greatest social experiments of the twentieth century. They matched up well to the belief in the potential of anyone to learn new and more adaptive ways of living with the necessary skills needed to shape new behaviors and without using coercive methods of threat or fear. These programs, based on strategies of reinforcement, produced results so spectacular that they were often referred to by patients, staff and families, as miraculous.

The application of the science of behavior is about how best to arrange conditions for learning to take place. Having seen what many families described as amazing changes in family members after years of suffering, and having seen equally impressive changes in behavior in the workplace, schools, and at home, these techniques should be used more often because of their efficiency and effectiveness in solving behavioral problems at all levels of society. By the way, they reduce human suffering in individuals and families as well.

Labels Are Not Behaviors *or* Life Sentences

To label someone is to put them in groups of similar individuals. It is easy and sometimes fun to categorize people. We need only go from the specific behavior to some more general, less-specific description. For example, many of us have been taught that a behavior like biting fingernails is not just a bad habit, but a symptom of an underlying problem such as insecurity. According to this school of thought, to do things to get the person to stop biting fingernails would be to ignore the underlying and thus deeper, more serious, problem. This widespread belief is straight out of Sigmund Freud's unproven work, work that has nevertheless permeated cultures around the world.

All of us have consistently occurring patterns of behavior that others call our *personalities*. This is a shorthand way of indicating who we appear to be. The important thing to remember about personality is that specific behavior patterns, while consistently expressed, "deeply engrained," or occurring habitually across many situations, can be changed. Try to imagine what a person could do if productive behaviors were developed to replace the troublesome ones.

Frequently, labels are used in ways that prevent those labeled from being seen as capable, or even to be given a chance to demonstrate their potential. Think of the descriptions you apply to yourself and try to be objective about what leads you or others to think in terms of your particular traits. Try to imagine how you would think of a person who irritated, annoyed, and bugged you if he stopped all those behaviors that you labeled irritating, annoying, or bugging and replaced them with behaviors that you considered helpful, cooperative, and considerate.

As we are able to identify and change small behavior patterns over time, it is quite possible to change personality. Behavior is fluid, surrounded by and part of a river of influence and effects. We are in constant motion every day of our lives, responding to and thereby being shaped by the conditions around us.

Personality may appear to be a deeper, more complete concept than a simple collection of behavior patterns, but if a person changed all their annoying or ineffective habits we could no longer maintain that their personality had not changed. Personality not only shows up in how you act or behave toward others but includes inconsistent behavior in different settings with different people, i.e., gregarious at home and quiet at work. Both patterns need to be considered when defining the "true" you. So, how do you change labels that have been applied to you that are based on the view that your personality is fixed? You change them one behavior at a time.

Labels: Changing How We Relate to Others

Words used to "explain" behavior bring overly complicated solutions to interpersonal problems while at the same time making such explanations too simple to understand causality. In fact, explanatory words about behavior most often lead to labeling once again. To say that a person lacks confidence and has an ego or self-esteem problem is too simple an explanation to be helpful. Such descriptions don't tell you what you should stop doing, start doing, or continue doing. To say that a person lacks confidence, one has to generalize from one or more behaviors to the label "lacks confidence."

A label of "lacking confidence" implies, wrongly, that the problem is an internal one for which the person somehow is either responsible or absent of direct responsibility. If the problem is perceived to be internal, most people are taught that "homemade" attempts to solve the problem might actually hinder a successful outcome, so we direct the person to a professional. However, when you understand that the problem is what you do, what you don't do, or how you do what you do, most problems can be dealt with directly as opposed to considering them to be "deep-seated" maladies. That is not to say that there are not multiple demonstrations of patterns of behavior that require professional help, but it is to say that not every nail-biter is anxious; nor does every stutterer have repressed sexual longings.

To say that a person is too emotional, too shy, too dependent, not a team player, or "too anything" is not helpful. To tell someone not to be so shy is less than helpful. As the saying goes, "Nothing is impossible for the person who doesn't have to do it." It is easy for a person who does not have these problems to tell others what to do. It is easy to tell a shy friend that he just needs to get over it, to just speak up, and so on. But your advice may appear way too simple and will likely be rejected because the person receiving the advice may think you don't understand his inner workings, thoughts, and feelings.

If a friend tells you that other people say you are "too negative" or "hostile," it is not helpful. You need help in identifying the specific situations or people who generate negative comments or reactions from you—something in those situations that you are reinforced for doing in their presence, that leads to a label about you that you want to change. You can then begin to look at your behavior more objectively. Methods for changing such patterns in ways that promote an honest but not hostile reaction will be introduced throughout this book.

Darnell's Case Study: Reading the Wrong Meaning into Behavior

If you are someone who takes great pride in your ability to "read" another person and their true intentions quickly, take a step back. Reading people and situations quickly based on our past perceived insight can often be wrong and lead to serious consequences for the other person.

Robert, an employee of a very large telecommunications company, worked his way up as a young technician in the field right out of high school, obtaining a college degree along the way. He had been with the company for 23 years and was being recognized for his hard work by being considered for promotion to a more senior-management position. Such advances were deeply coveted and much labor was spent in earning the position.

On the way to the final selection meeting, a woman on the committee overheard two people leaving another meeting, one a senior vice president who she respected very much. They were talking in animated terms about the importance of reaching agreement on the production issue they had been addressing and that Robert, while he was good at many things, was simply too stubborn to be a good team player. He simply would not compromise for the good of all on a matter of critical importance to the company.

The committee member went to her meeting and told the committee that she had it from a well-respected source that Robert, until then a strong candidate for promotion, was not flexible and did not compromise at critical times for the good of the company. She said, "I think he is not yet ready for a more senior leadership position."

No one on the selection committee asked a word about the context but accepted at face value the statements by the committee member. They had a lot of candidates to evaluate and they were not looking to add complications to the selection process. Robert was taken out of consideration for promotion but was told that he needed to work on his "team spirit," without any additional details. He soon left the company.

Robert's actions, that were labeled as uncompromising and not those of a team player, were actually that he refused to go along with a senior manager's argument in the meeting on production schedules that would compromise quality and safety. He was unwilling to budge in that instance because he truly thought it was harmful, thus demonstrating an admirable trait in the long list of attributes that made for an outstanding manager. This is an unfortunate but true story about the effects of labeling.

Back to the present. *Labels of all kinds are always a step away (in the wrong direction) from understanding the real problem.* If you use labels to define the cause of behaviors they so often fail because they don't help a person increase or eliminate behavior that leads to the label in the first place. Years can be wasted once people are saddled with a negative label. The act of labeling obscures behaviors and often puts a person in a box from which escape is difficult because no specific behaviors are pinpointed for change.

Assigning labels as more or less permanent parts of a person's personality does offer quick summaries of behavior patterns. We attach names to these patterns, allowing us to better understand, as we see it, the person as outgoing, rigid, humorous, shy, or careful. Some labels assign persons to groups that are considered inferior or of lesser worth and those who use such labels, in turn, expect performance that conforms to the stereotype. For example, to call someone a "Southerner" conjures up all kinds of labels: warm, friendly, slow, conservative, defensive, provincial, uneducated, and so on—yes, whatever you are thinking right now. The label may bias you to the point you would never hire a Southerner. However, if you live in the South, the label "Northerner" may conjure up arrogance, harsh judgment, and impatience.

On such factors alone, stereotypes of who a person is (or could be) are created based on labels formed from limited observations and personal assignment to a psychological label that no one really understands. Observe just one instance of your bias and then all such individuals assigned to that particular group are just as your labels told you they were.

Labeling causes us to miss seeing what the person is actually doing that is contrary to these stereotypes or that has its own value. We limit the human potential of another through labeling, an unwise choice for many reasons. Stereotypes or labels cause us to miss the very different but very rich human experiences of others, and, infrequently but still too often, justify extraordinarily harmful actions toward them. In casual conversation, we may all use summary descriptions, but they are not sufficient nor are they helpful when we are attempting to assess or change our behavior or someone else's.

No matter how wise we think we are, labels we use are not objective. Author Kate Long came up with a great book title that sums up the dangers of our lack of objectivity in assessing the causes of our neighbors', colleagues', or others' behavior patterns. The title of her book about children with developmental delays was based on a comment made by a pupil's teacher: *Johnny's Such a Bright Boy, What a Shame He's in Special Ed.*

Putting people in categories is almost never helpful in solving personal or work relationships. How helpful is it to conclude that a friend is depressed, anxious, schizophrenic, unmotivated, dumb, selfish, rude, or any number of other ways we use to describe him? Putting labels on people can be a serious matter. One of the problems is that when we put people in categories, we tend to treat them as though they *are* the category, but no one fits perfectly into any one category. Both of us (the authors) would qualify for the category *senior*, but neither of us thinks that we act like seniors are supposed to act. Once we are put into the senior category, however, if we forget a name, appointment, or place, others will attribute it to our declining faculties due to old age. If a younger person forgets the same kind of information, she simply says or thinks, "Everybody forgets."

If your child is diagnosed as having Attention Deficit Disorder (ADD) or is tested and found to be "gifted," it changes how you and others relate to that child. Some behaviors the "child with ADD" engages in, that you would have not responded to in a "typical child," are now viewed with suspicion and your behavior toward the child changes. Behavior (either good or bad) is interpreted and acted on based on the descriptive label attached to the child. Depending on the label placed on your child (*ADD* or *gifted*), you often don't know if you should ignore their behavior, stop it, or reinforce it.

You might think that a positive label would be acceptable. Not necessarily so. If you are told by a teacher that your child is smart, you may now believe the child understands many things you would have helped them with prior to the label. Now failure at a task may mean that the child is lazy, stubborn, or defiant when, in fact, he doesn't know how to accomplish the task. The assumptions about the meaning of any label lead to trouble. Ultimately, labels that lead to attributing cause to some internal and often misinterpreted, unchangeable pattern of behavior are generally unfair and create barriers to be overcome, even when they are positive.

Wonders of Being Human

Discussions about attribution and assumptions about capabilities may make it appear that scientific analysis of the human experience is limited, on a superficial level, to only that visible condition of speech and action. However, it is through speech and action that the very essence and deepest meaning about being human is found and shared.

Certainly, people are said to connect deeply to other human beings and that "deep" connection is achieved by their experiences through words and deeds. Profound feelings and deep emotions arise as a result of what people say and how they behave toward us.

Throughout the centuries, behaviors producing feelings of love and hate have been the genesis of inspiration for great music, poetry, art, or literature. Yet, when people are having difficulty with people who they once loved, or want to encourage expressions of warm affection from another, the way to help is to determine which behaviors need to occur more often, less often, or differently. Determining these behaviors requires that skill we discussed earlier as pinpointing, as boring or as dispassionate as that may sound.

Depth of passion, love and hate, artistic sensitivities, creativity, and innovation are all demonstrated in how we behave in particular environments, how we act toward one another, and how we speak to one another. Nevertheless (and this is equally important), it is not required to have a deep relationship with someone to help that person achieve deep and meaningful change. Novel patterns and extreme forms of human persistence can be explained through the science as well. Former president of South Africa Nelson Mandela, for example, was able to find or create reinforcers for behaviors that kept him focused on life during his 27-year prison sentence.[6]

Our most profound experiences as humans are not easily explained in terms of pinpoints found in specific events, but without those pinpoints, communicating profound experiences to others is difficult. Learning to describe those profound moments allows us to share in such experiences more completely. Our descriptive and sensory sensitivities are shaped by our histories of reinforcement.

The way our brain and our behavior interact to heighten certain sensory or other experiences often changes our physiological and physical actions. Memories return when the wind hits our face or a long forgotten song is played or a person walks by who looks just like our mother, producing changes in our expression, our emotions, and our actions—and all reflect on and enrich our experiences of interacting with our environment as human beings. We experience differing degrees of inspiration based on that history; an opera, soul food, classical and country music, the sound of a voice, rain on a tin roof, a soft touch, and so on. It is through the consequences we experience, one behavior at a time, that the depth of our human connection comes to be.

Once More with Feeling

Intense feelings are enriched as one learns how to describe and share such experiences with others. Feelings are often said to be the reason we experience what we do. (Nevertheless, how we describe our feelings in the presence of events or someone we love or hate is determined by the consequences we have experienced in the presence of such objects or people.) Feelings do not control us, rather it is our reactions to consequences that controls us and leads to the feelings we experience. Consequences change and the strength of our feelings change with them.

What we call great art and beauty are defined by consequences that shape our reactions. We certainly do not all describe the same reactions to various works of art nor do we all fall in love with the same person. That is a good thing. We find reinforcers in a thousand different things, developing physiological reactions to varied sounds and sights, taste, and touch. Those reactions, with words attached to describe them, like *love* and *hate*, *joy* and *despair*, come from our histories of reinforcement and current consequences that maintain or reduce the accuracy of the words we use to describe such feelings.

Private events—our thoughts and feelings—are defined through words, and they can be changed following the same scientific laws as does the more public behavior, which is most of what we write about in this book. Specifically, we are writing about the part of our behavioral repertoire that we all share. Those interactions are the sum total of how we know one another. We can share private thoughts directly by verbalizing or writing them, but until we do so, there is still no way to read another's thoughts and to know another person completely.

No test of internal brain function allows the neuroscientist or anyone else to read our thoughts, although specific parts of the brain light up (on an MRI or other medical device) when certain tasks are performed or depth of emotion is experienced. The fact that a part of the brain lights up when certain aversive conditions, words, sights, or sounds are introduced does not reveal what the person is thinking. All it tells us is that the two events are correlated. Evidence exists that the act of behaving, from eye movement to a raised hand to body posture, shows activity in parts of the brain. No one yet knows definitively the degree to which we are shaping our brain or our brain is shaping us, but our brains and our bodies respond interactively to consequences. Granted, without a brain, we would not be doing much of anything, so we are not suggesting that the brain is not relevant. Yet, for now, our thoughts remain private, and so we act on visible behavior.

As to emotions, we may observe physical changes in heart rate, sweaty palms, and a nervous stomach, but we cannot know the feelings and thoughts with which they are correlated except by some interpretation—and interpretation is filled with error. These physical responses may relate to thoughts of being deeply in love or to a dreaded public-speaking engagement. Physical reactions are in response to consequences for past behavior and anticipated future consequences. They are subtly or vastly different for every person. Love and hate can release the same biological triggers: sweaty palms, fast heartbeat, flushed face. However, what we do when in love is very different than what we do when angry or anxious. If we don't learn to discriminate among events that generate emotional reactions, we can behave in ways that do not match the events around us. We change our external behavior by mastering new skills, and that may change the words we say to ourselves and how we feel about the external events.

A lot of the angst of life is in the disconnection between how we feel or think and what we actually do or say that is accessible to others. Internal consistency with external behavior is important and cannot be discounted as a source of difficulty for people as they seek to change or engage differently with others. It is not enough to define us only by the things we say and do that are observable by others. Nevertheless, and of keen importance, to change public and private behavior, it is critical to learn to identify the conditions in which our behavior occurs and to provide different consequences to behave in ways that work well, reducing the report of troubling feelings or thoughts (Layng, 2009).[7]

Change the consequence to change the behavior, and its related feelings. Nothing that we propose negates the physiological and private patterns that promote living a more enriched and complete life. In fact, behavioral methods are designed to help people make positive and lasting changes in their lives to achieve a more complete sense of living a good life. As an example, Dr. Francis Mechner, director of the Queens, New York Paideia School, works to produce pinpointed patterns of behavior in his students that add up to what society calls *wisdom*.[8] He considers the ultimate measures of educational effectiveness as, *producing socially engaged graduates who have skills in considering the effects of their actions on the greater good of all and the development of a lifelong love of learning.*

The Importance of Being Precise

Our private world shapes and is shaped by our interactions with the external world. Learning how to navigate well through life depends on mastering the external demands required to achieve the lives we want. Day in and day out, the vast majority of us do just fine navigating through relationships and environmental requirements. Still, almost all of our problems boil down to one or more observable behaviors. We (they) do some things too often, some things too seldom or too little, or do the wrong thing(s). The problem is that we don't typically think of *behavior* because we have been taught to think more abstractly than in terms of specific action. In many social situations, it is inappropriate to talk precisely about behavior. A friend might say, "Have I told you about my problems?" Your response might be, "No, and I appreciate it." When someone asks, "How are you feeling?" to say, "Not too well: I have a stomach ache" probably communicates all that is necessary. More specific detail would be TMI (too much information)!

However, when we find ourselves with a problem, either with our own behavior or with that of another person, getting down to specifics is necessary for a quick and satisfactory solution.

The difficult part of solving most people's problems is determining the patterns of behavior that need to change. Once you know how to do this, and if you pinpoint the necessary changes, the actions to take are usually clear. Helping people determine how to set up the conditions that will solve a problem is a valuable skill and one that few people possess. Actually following through consistently with a plan is critical. Specifically describing needed behavior change has been seen by some as too cold, too insensitive, or too honest. On the contrary, learning to do so with clarity, in our view, creates compassionate and caring people.

Dispassionate Observation

Some people are better than others at accepting people without prejudging them. It is a great habit as they "never meet a stranger" and usually find aspects of interest in everyone they meet. As the character Forrest Gump said, "Life is like a box of chocolates. You never know what you're gonna get." Learning to know others by their words and actions is a skill more accurate than judging people by their appearance, such as their race, style of dress and tattoos. These differences can get in the way of knowing individuals for who they are.

Observing behavior across situations teaches more than does the first few minutes of interaction. Learning to be objective and to challenge your biases and beliefs is important in understanding your own and others' behavior. It is an essential skill and another requirement for determining the right pinpoints for change.

Look around and consider the descriptive names you have attached to those you have met or know well. Write down the pinpointed behaviors that you see them saying and doing that lead you to attach various labels to them. Consider carefully if the names you have attached limit what you expect of these people, even good friends. Finally, consider names or labels that have been attached to you. How do they help you, if they do, and how do the labels you know or assume others attach to you harm you?

Take these observations and identify the behaviors that lead you to say someone is shy, aggressive, a gossip, too intellectual, and so on. If you can identify one or two specific behaviors, you can start helping the person change so that even casual acquaintances will no longer use the label to characterize them.

Troubling labels limit your options. Remember the statement about Johnny? *"...such a bright boy, what a shame he's in special ed."* Think about it. Years ago we were testing children for eligibility for Vocational Rehabilitation services. A boy about age 10 came into the room, sat down and said, "If I do good on this test, will I be able to get out of Special Ed?" It was a heartbreaking moment because we knew that there was little the student could do to rid himself of the label that had been attached to him. It is clear that a label is limiting.

The irony in the title of Kate's book is alive and well. Test how you limit others. Return to the notion of specifically pinpointing the verbal and physical behavior you actually hear and see. Consider the circumstances that promote such activity. What can you do to arrange conditions to bring out the best in yourself and others? Every interaction changes the behavior of both parties. Therefore, the questions to be asked of anyone who seeks to change another are, "Do my interactions help this person? Am I inadvertently reinforcing behaviors that are problematic or am I reinforcing behavior that will help the person in interactions with others?" To arrange the conditions to bring out the best in that person, you will need the skill of *shaping*, the most important method of changing behavior you will ever have when interacting with another.

Know that when you engage in shaping you use positive strategies only—no threat and no fear. It is a liberating approach for you and the person you are working to help. It is respectful and often generates more positive reinforcement for you than for the person whose behavior has been shaped. Learning this skill and using it for the betterment of others can be one of the highlights of your introduction to the power of the science. We will discuss *shaping* in-depth in the following chapter.

4

How to Start Slow and Finish Fast

Ted Ayllon, a pioneer in behavior analysis, [9] gives his clients great advice: "Continue doing what you have been doing but make this *one small change*." In the fast-paced world that we live in today, asking for small changes seems out of place. How will we ever get to where we need to be if we settle for small changes?

However, by reinforcing small changes early you increase the rate of change later. Think of the launching of a rocket. If you have watched launches from the Kennedy Space Center, you will have noticed that after the rocket is fired it moves off the launching pad so slowly that you wonder if it will fall before it clears the pad. But even though it rises slowly in the beginning, within a minute or two it is traveling at thousands of miles per hour.

In a learning situation (behavior change), *positive reinforcement is to behavior as rocket fuel is to a rocket.* The rate of success or the rate of failure is determined in the *early stages*. If early responses produce frequent reinforcement, the rest is easy. If they don't, change is frustrating to the student and the teacher. Remember, a change agent's job is to make change easy and fun for the learner. In our learning centers in Atlanta, school children want to attend on Saturdays, Sundays, and even on holidays!

Each person defines what is positive (or negative) to him by what he does after receiving a consequence. It doesn't matter how much the person providing such reinforcement believes that it is positive. By definition, *positive reinforcement* must increase behavior or maintain it, or it is not positive reinforcement. This is a very important point if you are to use shaping successfully. Reinforcement cannot be found in a thing, a word, or an activity. It is found in how consequences impact a person's behavior. If the behaviors you are targeting actually increase in the future, they are being reinforced. If they do not, then what you thought was a reinforcer turns out not to be one.

Those who are best (most efficient and effective) in helping others change are those who can see and positively reinforce the smallest change that is trending in the right direction. That change may be slight indeed. The smaller, the better.

Constant State of Improvement

The process of *shaping* is formally defined as *the positive reinforcement of successive approximations toward the target behavior (goal)*. Successive approximations refer to many small steps toward the final version of behavior you are seeking. Behavior shaping requires that only positive reinforcement is used for even the smallest improvement. Focus only on improvement and remove all threat or fear from the situation. The reinforcers for making progress keep the next round going. The more reinforcement we get for small steps of improvement, the more steps a person achieves. Remember, learning should be a joyful experience.

If you ever had a teacher who found a way to consistently focus on the progress you made, no matter how small, then you remember the delight of learning in that environment. You knew when you made mistakes but the coach, teacher, or parent continued to focus on what you were learning, leaving you eager to learn more.

A common failure of people who are trying to teach or change behavior is to reinforce too little in the early stages. As described in the book, *Sidney Slug: A Computer Simulation for Teaching Shaping Without an Animal Laboratory*, Professor Loren Acker used a computer program, based on real-learning data from teaching animals in his lab, to teach shaping in a college course.[10] The task was to move Sidney, an animated slug, from one side of the computer screen to the other, as quickly as possible.

When Sidney moved, a click of the computer mouse, the reinforcer, would act to continue him on the same path. After having many students perform this task, Acker concluded that the most common failure was that the students were stingy. In their haste to move Sidney to the other side of the screen, they would require too much behavior before clicking the mouse, even though it cost them nothing. If they waited too long to reinforce, Sidney would move off track, veering to the left or right requiring extra time to get him back on track.

Another finding was that after Sidney got off track, the tendency of the students was to continue to wait until he moved in the correct direction. The problem was that, without reinforcement, Sidney would continue to move in all the wrong directions until his behavior was extinguished (he stopped). At this point, the task was discontinued as there was no behavior to move Sydney to the goal.

Dr. Acker taught students that sometimes, in changing behavior, you may need to start shaping behavior that is very different from the outcome or desired behavior you need, to be successful. Sidney, in heading to the left, could be shaped as he moved back toward the right direction without waiting for perfection. If Sidney continued moving in the wrong direction, some reinforcement to keep him moving was appropriate because if Sidney stopped moving altogether, no shaping (learning) was possible. Learning to provide generous amounts of PICs even for the smallest of steps in the right direction is one of the most important lessons, and for many the hardest, in using the tool of shaping.

The person interested in the well-being of others is an active seeker of the good that others do and is ready to reinforce even the smallest improvement in behavior. You can never go wrong reinforcing the smallest improvement that you can see. Those who do that see the fastest change.

When you withhold reinforcement because you have learned to save it until the end of a task or you worry that too much positive reinforcement is not good, you will rarely see accomplishment. Instead, you will see procrastination, lack of persistence, idleness, and resistance to your suggestions. Done correctly, you can never reinforce too often. Done incorrectly, one reinforcer is too many.

Being able to focus on the smaller steps toward the desired outcome requires a real understanding of how the learning curve occurs. It trends upward toward accelerated performance.

In the book, *Oops!: 13 Management Practices that Waste Time & Money*, "setting stretch goals" is the second of the 13 wasteful practices.[11] A stretch goal is set usually as a goal that is most often *quite a bit higher* than that of the last round of goal setting, and is an almost universal business practice. The goal is set at a level that causes the employees to "stretch" to meet it. The theory is that by asking for more than is reasonable, performers will accomplish more than the original goal.

As *Oops!* illustrates, research suggests stretch goals work only about 10 percent of the time. The reason stretch goals are a waste of time and money is that failure to reach a goal decreases motivation to try the next time, so that subsequent goals are taken less seriously or ignored.

Stretch goals continue to be used despite dismal results. One reason is that managers are positively reinforced for setting high goals. That intermittent reinforcement provided by even a low rate of success may be enough to continue an ineffective practice.

The real shame is that when stretch goals don't work, executives and other managers often punish people rather than look at management's failure to shape behavior. They often resort to negative reinforcement to reach their goals, which has a suppressing effect on the workplace culture well beyond the act of goal setting. That is, they use threat and fear to encourage achievement. *Do it or else* is a default management strategy with the result that managers reward a relative few and punish the many, reducing the overall rate of positive change inside their companies.

Managers frequently do not know how to build the stepwise acceleration into the environment that comes from clearly defined targets and the power of multiple reinforcement opportunities for achieving high-and-steady rates of performance. They do not practice *start slow and finish fast*. Starting slow may mean just setting aside a few hours or weeks to master new skills correctly versus starting fast and losing weeks or months focusing on off-target behavior.

Remember, *positive reinforcement accelerates the rate of responding*, punishment stops behavior, and negative reinforcement produces, *just enough to get by*. Referring back to the Discretionary Effort Model© in Chapter 2, company leadership could gain a lot by designing positive rather than negative approaches to human behavior if they want to achieve breakthrough performance. These same principles apply to home and family life, community, and social behavior—wherever initiating, accelerating, and sustaining change is needed.

Managers frequently do not know enough about how to build step-wise acceleration into the environment that comes from clearly defined targets and the power of multiple reinforcement opportunities for achieving high-and-steady rates of performance. They do not practice *start slow and finish fast*.

It is unfortunate that so few business schools teach the science of behavior to their future leaders. Most managers remain uninformed about how to reach goals by using behavioral principles. Failure to see this means that when goals fail, managers often punish people rather than look at management's failure to shape. When managers are taught to set a goal with a 10 percent success rate (stretch goals), they rarely ask meaningful questions about how to set those goals, but blame the performers when they are not achieved.

More importantly for business, the science shows how to set targets based on what we know about the rapid acquisition of new learning, so that employees managed in this way often exceed goals at levels that were once believed impossible!

Goals can indeed be set higher but the setting of an ultimate target is not the important part of goal setting. When the stretch goals are not achieved, managers often ask hard questions about their people, their lack of commitment and their drive. Rarely do leaders ask themselves if they set the wrong goal in the first place or more critically, if there are better ways to get to the results they desire.

Aubrey's Case Study: Setting the Right Goals

Mr. Grant, a former Army master sergeant, managed the cafeteria in a sheltered workshop for intellectually challenged children. The students spent most of the day learning to work in food preparation, auto maintenance and repair, and janitorial services, among other jobs. Students earned tokens for being on time, demonstrating appropriate behavior, performing assigned tasks, and for improvement on any personal behaviors necessary for employment. Tokens could be spent for playing games in a game room, breaks from work, and other activities that they valued.

One day Mr. Grant approached me (the behavioral consultant) concerning a problem student. He stated that this new student *would not do anything that he asked him to do.* If he told him to sit, he would stand. If he told him to stand, he would sit. If he tried to fool him by asking him to do the opposite of what he wanted him to do, he figured it out and still would not comply. A psychiatrist had diagnosed this student with the label "oppositional character."

I suggested that when Mr. Grant returned to the cafeteria, he should ask the student to bring him his token card and then give him enough tokens for 30 minutes in the game room. Mr. Grant responded, "I thought you taught us not to do that?" He was referring to the admonition not to give students tokens they did not earn.

I responded, "Since you want him to do what you ask, if he brings you his card when you ask, that is certainly a reinforceable response. The next time, however, ask *him* to add up the number of tokens he has and bring you his card so that you can see how many he needs to spend 30 minutes in the game room. After that, ask him to calculate the number he needs before going to the game room. It took less than one week until the student was performing all his duties in an exemplary fashion and the relationship between the two became extremely positive. In fact, the student was overheard saying to another instructor that Mr. Grant was his favorite teacher. To accomplish all of this, however, Mr. Grant's starting point was far from his goal. The lesson of setting goals is to start where the behavior is when you begin and set successive, small improvements (goals) from there.

Darnell's Case Study: Shaping Communication

I was at a university verbal-conditioning clinic working in a program designed to help children with speech issues. The shaping method was very precise, with measurement and recording occurring throughout the training.

Sam, a seven-year-old, was brought to the clinic by his parents. He didn't speak and made only grunting sounds. The sounds were loud, disruptive, and unpredictable. They were not in response to clear signals, did not seem to mimic normal speech, and were of such a pitch that most people wanted to be anywhere but near him. His vocal cords and hearing were normal. He started the grunting noises during the latter half of his first year. His parents needed relief in many areas but the grunting was difficult on the whole family, including Sam's two younger siblings.

Positive words alone had not produced any visible, measurable change in Sam's behavior. To shape from grunting to vocalization, food treats were used as reinforcers. I also hoped that my words would become reinforcers, in the moment, for needed behaviors. *In the moment* is critical, otherwise, with Sam or with anyone, a delay between the behavior and the reinforcer increases the probability that a behavior other than the behavior you want will be inadvertently reinforced.

To begin the training, Sam entered a small booth and sat across from me, looking everywhere but at me. These sessions were of short duration and occurred twice a day. Although cameras were on both of us, Sam did not look at or explore them. He made faces, drummed on the table, rocked back and forth and made the grunting sound for which he was famous. In the beginning, when he would turn his head toward me, usually with his eyes closed, I sought to reinforce "head turning" by providing him a small food treat at that moment. I kept at that until he was turning in my direction more and more, with his eyes still closed.

Any response that included turning of the head in the generally desired direction was reinforced. Sam began to turn his face toward my face at a high rate. He occasionally opened and quickly closed his eyes. When he turned and made a grunting sound, I reinforced the sound with food and also said, "*Good job turning your head.*" A counter was used throughout the training and the noise of the counter soon signaled good work in that only the correct movement was tracked. Grunting and head turning in the right direction continued to increase after that. Sam would blink his eyes open and shut and I would verbally reinforce the effort with, "*Good eye opening.*" Then I would say "*Ah*" as he faced me. When he made a grunting sound of whatever nature that approximated a *slight variation* on his usual sounds, I reinforced it. Then, as the responses came faster, I repeated the sound I wanted. At this point even slight variations in his vocalizations were reinforced.

Soon, Sam was coming to the session, looking at me, and saying a sequencing of sounds and words formally introduced in the session. Mastering these sounds would be needed if he were to speak clearly to others. At the middle of the third week, grunting had disappeared during the sessions.

During this time every approximation to the behavior I needed was reinforced. I kept eye contact so Sam could see my face and watch my mouth make sounds that he then made that were moving in the right direction. All other distracting behaviors were ignored, gaining neither praise nor punishment. By the fourth week, Sam was making many sounds. He began repeating two-word phrases and *suddenly* it seemed he was repeating back full sentences (three to five words). He learned to answer and to ask his own questions. He could describe simple things he did during the day like throw a ball or play with his stuffed bear.

With his parents, however, Sam still grunted. When the therapy continued in an outpatient setting (his home), a program was designed to help him generalize appropriate responses to his parents, and in various community settings (for example, the mall, fast-food restaurants, church, and school). Before too long, he was asking rudimentary questions and responding with short answers in a number of settings. The grunting disappeared except on rare occasions.

His language skills required years of continued training in a classroom with a behavior-analytically trained speech therapist and teacher where he began to use more complex sentences and spontaneous conversation. It sounded halting and was not always timely or appropriate, but he was a boy who learned to speak after his parents were certain that this life skill was not going to happen.

While this kind of astonishing change is happening at behavior-based autism spectrum centers across the world today, in the 1970s such quickly adaptive skill acquisition was unheard of. Most children with severe development disabilities and autism were not thought to benefit from training or therapy. Dr. Ivar Lovaas, as evidenced in the previously mentioned film, *Reinforcement Therapy*, showed that children who were severely disabled could make amazing changes.[12] His work was extremely successful and today, his basic technique continues to be used in thousands of clinics worldwide. Unfortunately, many non-behavioral centers still do not use this powerful technology.

Learning how to shape correctly is the most important behavior-change skill you can have as a parent, teacher, coach, manager or executive. Anyone who has this skill has the potential to influence the behavior of others. Shaping creates independence and robust capabilities. Shaping arises from the science of learning and is the most effective technique in the toolkit of behavior change. If you are good at shaping, you will be continually surprised at what others can learn. You will be surprised at how it shapes you to see behavior differently. However, to be effective, you must be generous in providing rapid and timely reinforcement for *any* progress.

This is the technique that converted both of us to use the phenomenal power of positive reinforcement (PICs) to change all kinds of behavior quickly to increase positive outcomes. We have used this knowledge in clinical practice, in schools, and in businesses for more than 40 years. Like the Midas touch, this approach gave our clients real skills that changed their lives and their businesses in fundamental ways.

Oh, and we never did find out why the child grunted or the student did the opposite of what was asked because we knew all we needed to know from observing their behavior. As their behavior was shaped toward more functionally and socially appropriate behavior, it led to more and more natural reinforcers. What we did know is that they behaved and were responded to in different ways, leading to fuller lives.

Guidelines for Shaping

You can tell *most* people about the change process, the behaviors you want to see, and how you will be working with them to get to the end goal. For others, such as children with severe autism, how and if you describe your actions depends on the language skills of the child. These nine points are crucial to success in shaping behavior:

1. Pinpoint the outcome and the behaviors the person needs to perform that will help achieve the goal down the road.

2. Do not use threat, fear or punishment; only use positive reinforcement whenever you shape.

3. At first, positively reinforce any improvement, no matter how small, as soon as you see it.

4. Find an effective reinforcer, one that produces a response in the desired direction.

5. Immediately reinforce any behavior that represents progress toward the outcome you desire.

6. Focus on the learner and his behavior and give your attention generously and immediately when you see any behavior approximating what you want.

7. If necessary, prompt responses, even if the response seems far removed from the ultimate behavior you want, and then immediately reinforce the response to the prompt.

8. Withdraw prompts as the behavior becomes frequent.

9. Continue to reinforce from time to time (intermittently) even when the final outcome has been achieved.

Admittedly, shaping can be challenging to do, yet it is invaluable. Shaping done well allows for quick skill acquisition in things like learning to ride a bike with support until wobbling stops or tying shoes, and advancing to more complex behaviors like learning to play the piano. Taking on increasingly complex legal writing, learning to play soccer or writing music are all skills best acquired through shaping. All college courses are best learned through shaping. It is not just a way to teach the most basic behaviors and skills, but any complex activity or information by people of all ages.

When applying these steps to goal setting, look at the goal from the vantage point of the outcome that is desired and think about approximations to achieve the desired result. If the learner plateaus, break the task into smaller parts until progress continues. If the individuals move at a rate faster than you planned, do not increase the requirement necessary for reinforcement. Each visible success toward the outcome is a reinforcer for most people. Observing and commenting on specific behaviors is usually reinforcing as it lets the performer tell you or one another how they are achieving such success. All those things are, for most of us, highly reinforcing.

If you are having difficulty finding a reinforcer that might work for a new behavior you want, remember that many things serve as reinforcers and most of us can find common ground in that vast array of potential reinforcers. Knowing what you know about the individual, you cannot hurt them by making the environment more naturally reinforcing or by initiating social and other changes that look like they will work.

There are many generalized reinforcers that, to varying degrees, most people respond to *positively*. Use them and watch what happens to the person's behavior. Your efforts to reinforce progress are essential, but they are often not the only or even the most important sources for sustaining behavior change. An endless supply of reinforcers is available in life to sustain new behavior. Your job is to create the conditions that allow the person to earn those reinforcers.

If at work, where performers set their own goals, encourage them to set many small steps or sub-goals so that they get a lot of reinforcement early in the process. Those early goals should be set so that the person can be successful 100 percent of the time. Be careful though. Individuals and teams, having success in the early stages, often begin to set subsequent goals too high. It is often the job of the parent, teacher, or coach to make sure that the goals continue to be achievable so that reinforcement will continue to be forthcoming. That means in some cases you may need to say something like, "I like the way you are thinking, but for now I will be happy if you accomplish this much (a reduced amount)."

As long as you understand that it is not the goals that are important but 1) the steps to get there, 2) what happens along the way, and 3) what happens after the goals have been achieved, you and those you work with will be successful in achieving exponential change at home, at school, and in the workplace.

Remember that the possibilities for the most-skilled student are also possibilities for the least-skilled student if that student has a good teacher. Shaping is an essential skill of teachers to create as much independence and mastery of skills as possible by their students. Shaping new skills is ubiquitous in cultures around the world. It occurs every day and is the fuel for learning the skills we need in this life.

When behaviors are specified clearly and concretely to achieve desired results, the opportunities for positive reinforcement increase at each step along the way. A very helpful tool to become more systematic about how to create strategies for positive results is called the Five-Step Model of Behavior Change, introduced in the next chapter. It provides an objective, science-based method for evaluating and refining any change strategies.

5

Five Steps to Behavior Change

In the 1960s, Dr. Ogden Lindsley, a psychologist at the University of Kansas, created a very effective process to help parents solve family and relationship problems.[13] According to Dr. Lindsley, data from hundreds of applications showed that those parents who followed his model solved their problems 98.6 percent of the time. Over the last 40 years we have changed the model slightly and applied it successfully in solving thousands of business problems. Many managers, having success with this model at work, applied it with equal success to problems at home, with their own behavior, and even in their communities. This model works as well in designing plans to help children achieve positive results with homework, friendships, hobbies, or social interactions with the adults around them.

In the model, two areas are always monitored: 1) the outcomes or results you want and 2) the specific behaviors required to achieve those results. In business, a result may be to achieve profits. In raising children, a result may be a clean room.

Pinpointing: The Process of Being Specific About Results and Behaviors

First, identify the outcomes or results you want as specifically as you can. Results can be, "Increased Quality" for a business and "Clean Room" for a parent. Once the results have been determined, the behaviors necessary to create those results need to be identified. One of the behaviors that increases quality may be "cleaning the equipment before starting." At home, the behaviors of cleaning a child's room may be "picking up dirty clothes and placing them in a hamper" and "making the bed by pulling the blanket up to the pillow," as part of a checklist called, "clean room."

The process of being specific about behaviors and results is called *pinpointing*. Many of the words listed on the non-behavior side of the table on the next page appear to be what we typically call behavior but are in fact labels, a sum-up of what we think the behavior signifies. Behavior is a much more specific event than what the non-behavior words suggest. The totality of behavior leads to the application of such words. We often call someone "innovative" or "devious" based on how we have come to understand such words. However, to understand how to increase or decrease things you do or don't like, you must be very clear about what the actual behaviors are that you can see people saying and doing.

In our work, considerable time is spent helping students learn to observe and precisely pinpoint the behavior that they see and hear. In solving behavioral problems this is definitely worth the time. Learning to look first, before making judgments, is a difficult but valuable skill to acquire. Thomas Gilbert, author, professor, and student of B. F. Skinner said, "Look before you listen." Since we all put our spin on what we relate to others, the best way to make sure that we identify the target behaviors of interest is to see them for ourselves.

Non-Behaviors and Behaviors

Behaviors are what we see a person saying and doing. Non-behaviors are often attributes or a summary word we apply to a pattern of behavior that might have varied meaning. When pinpointing what needs to change or improve, it is important to be as specific as possible so that small changes can lead to real improvement.

Non-Behavior	Behavior
Ambitious	Eating
Competencies	Hitting
Concentrating	Kissing
Creative	Lifting
Devious	Painting
Engagement	Running
Helpful	Shaking hands
Innovative	Singing
Helping	Stopping a car
Lazy	Talking
Enthusiastic	Crying
Managing	Tying your shoes
Paying Attention	Typing
Responsible	Walking
Smart	Writing
Studying	Hugging
Supervision	Laughing
Reading a book	Smiling
Learning	Reading a book out loud
Being happy	Describing a sunset
Feeling sad	Turning
Truthful	Looking down

While interpretations about the meaning of behaviors we observe are perhaps more satisfying than an unemotional description of behavior, the latter is infinitely more useful in resolving an individual's problems or habits, or in identifying patterns of success.

We *are* our behavior. The only way people know us is by what we say and do; that is, our behavior. Many nonscientific commentators on the human condition have concluded that we are more than our behavior, that the deeper we go inside our psyches the more likely we are to discover who we really are. When advice givers on TV and in print tell people they need to "find themselves," what could they mean? Or when people are told to "be your authentic self," what does that mean? If you are considered to be shy by your family and friends, does that mean you should just "own it" and express your shyness? If you are really selfish and think the world is all about you, does that mean that you should "own that authentic part of yourself" and act that way without regard for what people think or feel about you? You don't need to go deep inside the arrogant person to know that you don't want to be around that guy or have any dealings with him.

If "go deeper" means take the time to consider your thoughts, feelings, dreams, and aspirations that you rarely, if ever, discuss with others, we would certainly agree. As we discussed in Chapter 3, such content is important to the fullness of your individual life, but of course, they are private events, not observable to others. It is quite possible that your thoughts (private behavior) may be different from your public behavior, but in the final analysis, your private behavior counts little in terms of how people relate to you or what their opinion is about you. It counts little because no one else can know it. What you say and do in the presence of others is public. Your thoughts, feelings, dreams, and aspirations become visible and are subject to change, once others witness them through your actions.

Not all behavior needs to change. In many circumstances, wide ranges in behavior are acceptable, and even desirable (for example, skill in solving novel problems). Even if you don't like what or how someone says or does things, pick the targets for change carefully. Analyze the effects of current patterns at least by considering whether your standard of correctness need apply to the behavior of others. For example, we authors don't understand the attraction of tattoos. Perhaps it is because we are older, but more likely it's because of our behavioral histories. We can advise but we are rarely, or truthfully never, asked to express our opinion about the potential unintended consequences and long-term effects of getting a tattoo, unless it is for one of our own children or family members. Of course, and importantly for all of us to remember, social context changes and we are finding that the next generation is more fully accepting of tattoos, and a new social norm is generalizing well beyond the authors' particular histories of reinforcement.

That is the thing about judging the behavior of others outside the ever-changing social context of their own histories. Families attempt to shape children to their social standards. As family standards vary rather widely among millions of families worldwide, this guarantees that a diversity of behavior will always be with us.

How people look or act can make us uncomfortable but the real test is, does their behavior get in the way of effective and efficient work or socially responsible behavior? Or would it cause harm to self or others? Finding our judgment clouded by our own discomfort is a large part of how biases essentially blind us from seeing the individual apart from our stereotype. Generalizing, and a failure to pinpoint actual behavior, keeps the stereotype going.

Pinpointing is necessary for delivering useful feedback and effective consequences. The establishment of a behavior pinpoint is critical to the collection of data to analyze what you did and its effect on desired outcomes. It allows you to teach and coach more effectively and for quicker learning to occur. If you are the learner, consider how much easier it is when the expectations and the steps to get there are specified in performing a new task. Think of the times you have tried to put a gadget together that came from a foreign country written by non-native English writers, for example, or written by English writers who assumed certain steps didn't need to be explained.

As you delve into this subject, the chart below provides good questions to ask to become even better at the critical skill of pinpointing. In conjunction with this checklist, the result, or end-goal, must be made clear in order for you to know where you are going.

Most people have little difficulty defining the desired outcome. However, behavior is different. Many things are considered to be behavioral pinpoints that are actually outcomes—internal mood ("I need to get happy"), emotional triggers ("I don't want to be afraid in front of the classroom"), or a moral standard ("I want to show more concern for others"). What do attributes such as "happy," "not afraid," and "show concern" look like? What would we want to see these people do to create these outcomes? An important point related to pinpoints is that stopping a negative behavior is rarely an effective way to solve a problem.

Checklist for Evaluating a Pinpoint

Directions: Answer yes or no to each question. If you have an accurate pinpoint, all the answers to questions 3 through 7 should be YES. Modify the pinpoint for a NO answer. If you can't correct the pinpoint, drop it and get a new one.

PINPOINT:		
	Yes	No
1. Is it a result?*		
2. Is it a behavior?*		
3. Is it measureable?		
4. Is it observable?		
5. Do two independent counts usually agree?		
6. Is it under the performer's control?		
7. Is it an active performance?		

*If it is not a behavior or result, it is probably not a pinpoint.

To quote Yogi Berra, the Baseball Hall of Fame catcher and master of wonderful misquotes, "If the fans don't come out to the ballpark, you can't stop them." State the pinpoint in active terms. What can you do that addresses the problem behavior? Defining the behavior you want instead of the behavior you don't want leads to more positive solutions. Rather than tell a child to stop leaving clothes on the floor, you reinforce the behaviors of hanging clothes in the closet and putting them in the dresser drawer. With these behavior pinpoints, fussing at the child becomes unnecessary.

Important, but hard-to-pinpoint behaviors that people want from others are at times stated as generalized values ("do greater good to others" or as a stop doing, a *non-behavior*, like "stop lying"). If you can specify when lying occurs, you can change the conditions so that truth telling is reinforced. "Do greater good" may be an overarching result but it is not a behavior.

The behavioral pinpoint for doing greater good may be to "volunteer to pack food at the local food bank once a week." If that meets the *doing good* criteria for the person who defined it, it is one way to demonstrate that poinpoint. A good behavioral pinpoint is one that is measurable, observable, active, under the performer's control, and reliable (in that two or more people could agree if the activity occurred or did not). The final question you might ask is, "Is it valid? Does this behavior for a food bank really do greater good?" On its face, it does.

In addition to task completion in the manner needed, your outcomes can produce not only objective results but various values-based or subjective results such as satisfied customers or a happy mother. Any result you want to achieve needs to be specified clearly, if you are to begin to pinpoint the behaviors that are required to get there.

Once you have pinpointed the result, carefully pinpoint the behaviors required to achieve those results. This can be whole patterns of behavior, like those required to teach a child to make a bed or pick up clothes, all the way to specific behaviors in monitoring, maintaining, and fixing equipment required to produce and ship products on time in a business supply chain. They can include behaviors you want to increase by using the effects of consequences to guide you. In the workplace or at home, skills are often learned one behavior at a time. Remember what you learned about completing a PIC/NIC Analysis® and consider how to design PICs to attain and sustain desired behavior.

We have spent considerable time writing about the first step in the Five-Step Model of Behavior Change—*pinpoint*—a critical and perhaps the most difficult step to get right, but it requires the rest of the model to be complete. Consider now the whole model when approaching change:

Step 1. **Pinpoint**—identify the results (outcome) and specify the behaviors needed. Step 1 is the most time-consuming part of the process, but done correctly, significantly sets up the right course for change. Once you complete this first step of specifying results and the behaviors required to get there, then use the following four steps of this Five-Step Model to calibrate and make sure you are doing all you can—not only to get behavior going but staying, to the point where, for example, bed making (or any other desired behavior and result) is maintained to a standard that becomes "just the way things are done around here."

Step 2. **Measure**—develop a way to track (record) any changes in both behavior and results. Today many apps can help track both. Try to track the occurrence of events with discrete numbers rather than with a subjective judgment, as in good, better, best or rating against some standard or scale (rate your pain on a 0-to-10 scale). It is not that these measures are not helpful, but when learning new or discrete tasks, judgment is less accurate compared to actually counting the occurrences, such as the discrete measures[7] of every step you take on the Fitbit or other device when walking to improve your health.

Step 3. **Feedback**—while specific words do create powerful and often immediate feedback valued by many performers, we suggest that you create a way to display the data so that the changes are visible to you and the performer(s). We are likely to ask, "Can you put it on a graph?" A graph shows you where you are, where you've been, and where you need to be. It is a lasting and visual record of accomplishment and can serve as a more permanent way to deliver feedback. Verbal feedback is often misheard or not heard at all, or if heard, is quickly forgotten. This can limit the amount of positive reinforcement associated with it. If you post a graph, all who see it can comment on it, potentially providing social reinforcement.

Step 4. **Consequate**—arrange consequences to increase desired behavior. Again, focus on having behavior that you want to increase. Because positive reinforcement is the best consequence to use to increase behavior, select a reinforcer that you have observed to work in other situations. Also, choose a positive reinforcer that can be used frequently. You can help yourself or others develop excellent habits when, in the early stages, the behaviors produce high rates of PICs as evidenced by the ways in which behavior changes in the desired direction.

Step 5. **Evaluate**—examine the results to see if your plan is working. First, look at the result to see if it has changed in the desired direction. Then look at the behavior to see if it has increased. If the behavior has not changed, chances are that you do not have an effective reinforcer and you should try another positive reinforcer. On the other hand, *if the behavior has changed but the result has not, you have learned that the behavior you have pinpointed is not crucial to the results.*

Being this systematic about solving people's problems produces high rates of success. Ogden Lindsley's data showed that if the first attempt doesn't, trying one or two more times with precision almost always solves the problem. The model is simple to implement and we train people to follow the steps faithfully until they have become fluent in using it.

Importance of Trial and Success

We are often asked to talk about where this method was applied and didn't work. Our facetious answer is "If you can tell us a place where gravity didn't work, we will tell you a place where the laws of behavior didn't work." Of course we have had situations where we didn't get the results we wanted, but we have never had a situation where someone followed the process and the process didn't work.

As some readers have noticed, the Five-Step Model is a variation of the scientific method. In science, the secret to success lies in large part in the adage, "If at first you don't succeed, try, try again," while following the same process systematically as you vary the conditions you are examining. Our confidence comes from working with thousands of people in the home and in the workplace to solve problems that had plagued the families and the businesses for years.

The series of questions in the table on the next page can help you assess whether or not you are correctly identifying and applying the elements of the Five-Step Model to achieve the results you seek. As we stated earlier, the Five-Step Model contains the core elements of the scientific method. When you use it, think of it as representing the scientific method to ensure you are being objective and evaluative as to whether you are producing the right results for the person(s) and the situation.

Questions to Ask to Achieve Behavior Change

Using the Five-Step Model:

1. Pinpoint
a. What specific result do you want to achieve?
b. What specific behaviors will help you achieve those results?

2. Measure
a. How will you know when you reach the result?
b. How will you   track the behaviors?

3. Feedback
a. Can you put results and behaviors on graphs?

4. Consequate
a. Performance consistently above goal?
b. Are behaviors increasing?

5. Evaluate (continuous cycle during change process)
a. Did you achieve the result?
b. Did the targeted behavior increase as results increased?

© 2017-2020 Aubrey Daniels International, Inc. www.aubreydaniels.com

---

More details of the Five-Step Model are included throughout this book for designing, developing, and monitoring more effective patterns of behavior. The model as an embodiment of the scientific method becomes a ready checklist for anyone attempting behavior change.

In the first chapter we introduced a decision tool, the PIC/NIC Analysis®, which you can use to examine the consequences that are accelerating, maintaining, or hindering human behavior and to arrange the type, timing, and certainty of consequences to bring about positive change. By rearranging the environment, you can be an agent of positive change. That is where the consequences reside that motivate behavior. We then examined how our biases and assumptions, used to describe others, can hinder a clear-eyed view of what people are capable of doing. Next, we learned that shaping is a critical tool for arranging positive change and that the Five-Step Model helps us be accountable for what we do to help in that change. However, it is not our good will or our good intentions that cause that change.

What motivates the change? Once you begin to see that behavior changes rapidly when positive techniques are applied, in steps along the way, you are getting closer to understanding what comprises behavior and are on the way to understanding the sources of its motivation. However, one thing is true. We all too often get motivation wrong.

6

Motivation Is an Outside Job

A very large part of the population believes that the source and solution to most problems is internal—an attribute of the person's personality rather than what the person does in the external environment. As with the biases of a fixed personality and various labels used to describe that personality, many believe that people cannot be changed by simply arranging external conditions. They think motivation has to come from within despite the fact that consequences follow a lawful pattern to generate, accelerate, and maintain behavior. Here is how such a belief generates assumptions that direct us away from examining motivational factors in human behavior.

As we discussed in Chapter 3, if we label someone as depressed, lazy, insecure, rude, or driven, the focus is on the person as the offender. If the problem is conceptualized as internal, it is almost impossible to change someone's behavior, because we would have to change the person's internal processes. To help people change with only this level of understanding requires that we read their minds. This is not possible: not by clinically trained psychologists, psychia-trists, or even neuroscientists.

We tend to interpret the person's behavior. For example, if you attribute a person's failure to complete his work on schedule as being caused by his "laziness" you would do better to look to the environment for causes of the behavior. However, when the problem is defined behaviorally, as in, "he doesn't complete his work on time," no labels are needed. Then you can begin to help him through the managerial responses and workplace conditions by providing PICs for efforts directed toward completing activities on time or even early. Soon, he will be known as a person who does complete his work on time. Again, no labels are needed! Being lazy need never be discussed again.

When so-called body language experts are asked to analyze the body language of people in the news, even though they have been "trained" to do this, their interpretations are about as reliable as the readings of a roadside fortuneteller. Although we are looking at what people say and how they say it (including mannerisms and body posture), ascribing mental activity such as feelings and intent is highly unreliable. When asked what the crossed arms of a listener in a presentation means, many people will tell you that it means the person is closed to the ideas being presented. Nonethe-less, many other interpretations are possible, such as the person is cold and keeping her arms close to her body to keep warm, or that this is simply a position that is comfortable. Even those assumptions cannot be made reliably.

We have seen many times that the person in a training class who looked like she was the most interested turned out to be paying the least attention, and the one who looked not only uninterested but angry about being in the class turned out to be the friendliest, the first to express gratitude for all he had learned, and the first to apply it to his work. In the end, the real meaning of behavior can be found by observing what the person actually does.

Intentions Lost in Well-Intended Translation

Reading intention into people's actions is so common because we think we know what we are observing and we also think we know its meaning. Such reading of someone's intention does nothing to teach us how to shape, guide, and support behavior change. This attempt to read the intention into one's body position and expression is the source of much unhappiness in relationships as well.

We think we can read people we are close to because we may have had a history with them, and when they talk and act in a particular way, we are able to predict reasonably well what they are feeling or thinking. This is because we have had many opportunities to observe their behavior and informally correlate it with outcomes. We get in trouble when we see those same behaviors in someone we just met, or only know casually, and assume that their behaviors mean the same as they do with someone we know better. Jack Webb, as Detective Sergeant Joe Friday in the popular 1960s television series, *Dragnet*, stated our position well when he said in almost every episode, "Just the facts, ma'am."

What is the person doing? What behavior would be better? Stick to the facts regarding what you can actually see. Don't interpret.

By sticking to overt behavior, anything you can hear people saying or see them doing, avoids mindreading or other forms of "figuring people out" based on faulty interpretations of what they do. Because behavior is active, observable, measurable, repeatable, and reliable, people can look to behavior to determine what is working and what is not.

Objectivity: A Friend in Science

Many people treat family members in ways that they would never treat co-workers. That variability is what makes the observation of behavior so important. Behavior occurs in an environment that contains a person's history of reinforcement and the current consequences. The appropriateness of the behavior is determined by the effects it has in a given situation.

At times we all have trouble objectively seeing or hearing what others are saying or doing without trying to interpret it. We are so often wrong. For example, when we conclude from a first impression that we *know* the person. Whatever the assumption-driven and generally wrongheaded research might tell you about what you can learn in the first moments of introduction, those impressions arise from only a small sample of the person's behavior and capability. If that were not so, why is it that business people make so many poor hiring decisions?

Remember, your prior learning biases what you see and what you think you know about another person and the world around her. Even though the formerly popular television commentator, Bill O'Reilly, talked about the "No Spin Zone," no such thing or place really exists. As we have noted several times, we all are the beneficiary *and* the victim of our past experiences, which shape our behavior, habits, beliefs, and prejudices.

We cannot just walk away from our habits, beliefs, and prejudices, or act as though they don't exist. But they can be changed by what we say and do and by the consequences in the situations in which we find ourselves. As Mark Twain said, "Habit is habit and not to be flung out of the window by any man, but coaxed downstairs a step at a time." That one step at a time occurs at a fast trot once we understand how to accelerate the process of behavior change.

The question to ask when trying to help someone solve a behavior problem is, "What is the problem?" which should be followed by, "What does that look like?" What does *confidence* look like? What does *engagement* look like? When you see a person you have confidence in or who is engaged in her work, what would you see that person do? In the end, it always comes down to "What precisely do you want her to do?" When you answer that question, the change is already half done. It is the hardest and most time-consuming part of problem solving. It is about seeing behavior in terms of the effects of that behavior. It is in this external view that we find both the desired outcomes we want and the motivation to start and continue behavior change.

Although many motivational speakers, authors, and professors write and preach that motivation is an inside job, behavior analysis tells us that motivation is more usefully thought of as an *outside* job. Reliance on internal states of belief or desire, willpower, innate talent, intelligence or lack thereof, or other notions of why we do what we do puts the responsibility for change inside the other person.

The truth is that the person we want to change is doing something other than what we want, but as far as she is concerned she is doing just fine. The child who doesn't respond to the parent's call to dinner does not have a problem in continuing to do what he is doing. The employee does not have a problem with doing minimal work. Both may have a problem with how people react to them or what they tell themselves about their performance, but they do not have a *problem* in doing what they do. They do it just fine. They may not respond to calls from parents or they may not do the work on time. However, they continue doing what they do. It is the parent or employer who is unhappy with the behavior of the child or employee. Until there is a change in the conditions surrounding the behavior, it will continue and the parent and employer will continue to be unhappy.

Motivation is the spark for change. If we learn how to arrange outside conditions to motivate behavior change in addressing a variety of critical human problems, the effects multiply rapidly through the ongoing effects of PICs. The old ways haven't worked very well in changing individuals or addressing the larger problems of the world. Change is possible and certainly occurs, but there is not sufficient understanding of how to set up conditions for lasting social and cultural changes.

Consequences—Persuasive and Powerful

Understanding the outside/inside notion requires that we understand the power of consequences. The PIC/NIC Analysis® helps us analyze what kinds of consequences are operating on us as we say and do things. Understanding the various types of consequences is the key to using the information found in a PIC/NIC Analysis®. Understanding the following facts about consequences and their motivational effects for increasing, decreasing, or maintaining behavior will help you to better understand how to change behavior.

There are four behavioral consequences: Positive reinforcement, negative reinforcement, punishment, and penalty. All are effective in changing behavior. As stated earlier, a *behavioral consequence* is by definition not a "consequence" unless it changes behavior.

More about consequences:

- **Positive reinforcement** increases behavior without threat or fear. It accelerates the rate of responding and increases the positive effects of learning.
- **Negative reinforcement** can increase behavior but at a cost. People do what they do under this condition to

avoid or escape punishment or the threat of punishment. It creates a condition where people improve, but
often do just enough to avoid punishment.

- **Punishment**, including penalties, stops behavior. A
  significant problem with the use of punishment is that
  those delivering punishment are often positively
  reinforced by the immediate change in the other person's behavior (PIC) resulting in the accelerated use
  of punishment to solve problems. Negative reinforcement and punishment are not the same. They have the
  opposite effect on behavior. Punishment stops behavior. Negative reinforcement increases or maintains
  behavior, but often not at maximum rates once the
  threat or avoidance situations are removed.

- **Extinction** begins when behavior occurs and it
  receives no reinforcement. Behavior that is not reinforced in any way and eventually stops under this
  condition is said to have been extinguished. There is
  much interest currently in the research literature about
  the process of extinction and what is happening over
  time. Generally, what we know is that if you ignore a
  behavior that has been reinforced by your actions, the
  behavior will gradually reduce in frequency in your
  presence and will eventually stop. However,
  extinction takes time and a disciplined approach by the
  one who is ignoring specific behavior. It requires
  many occasions without reinforcement for a behavior
  to stop under extinction, but extinction is often chosen
  as an alternative to punishment. Ignoring the behavior
  you do not want, if it is not dangerous or harmful in
  other ways, while reinforcing alternative behavior that
  is or approaches the behavior you want, allows you to
  attend in positive ways to behaviors that you consider
  more appropriate for the person while being diligent
  in ignoring problematic behavior.

- Behavior that increases or is maintained over time is being reinforced, no matter how the consequence appears to others.
- Small, immediate consequences are more powerful than larger, delayed ones.
- In establishing new behaviors, consequences that are certain to occur have more impact on behavior than those that are uncertain.
- Telling, yelling, and showing in the absence of consequences has unpredictable effects on behavior. Used so often in management and parental practices, they all occur *before* behavior change and are technically called antecedents. Although often they are considered to be motivational, they have little to no effect on behavior unless followed by a behavioral consequence.
- Telling people about consequences that will follow a particular behavior or condition is not a consequence.
- Doing something (words and actions) and coming in contact with effective consequences are at the heart of designing effective behavior change.

Urgent Need for Enlightenment

Basic scientific principles of behavior and their sources of motivation, easily extracted through a thorough PIC/NIC Analysis® can immediately begin to have positive effects in how we solve our personal and people problems. As with any science, there is still much to learn about why people behave the way they do, but there is also much that we do know.

The principles discovered are the same for all of us, independent of culture, age, sex, national origin, or personal history. PICs and NICs occur in every culture, with any age, across gender, or histories of learning. They open the gateway to understanding why we each act as we do.

The science of behavior can be used to solve many problems that have complicated our lives and plagued the world for centuries. Knowing these principles and applying them skillfully creates the possibility of achieving extraordinary change in the human condition. As you read on, you will see the value of these principles in your own life and will understand how you can put them into action.

There is a belief among those who study behavior that human behavior is unlimited in its potential. There are some natural limits of physiology or the variety of experiences influencing choices. Nevertheless, in general and across the widest range of behavior, human potential is virtually unlimited if the right conditions exist. When you think of another person's potential, even your own, think of possibilities rather than limitations. The science tells us that, almost everyone is capable of much more than is being realized.

Part II

Spheres of Influence: Potential, Environmental, and Values-Based

7

Unleashing Human Potential

We have talked a lot about one's potential, but can we really know the potential of another? If we use shaping or any other change strategy, don't we need to know more about the person we are trying to change? Don't we need to know how personal history and achievement thus far have affected that potential? Don't we have to know what the person believes about himself...his self-worth? Actually, we don't.

We must know that potential is, in essence, unleashed by an environment designed to reinforce learning. When that kind of environment exists, the accomplishments are often off the charts. Unfortunately, most students do not have such an environment. That is what shaping can do. Let's see how biases about potential can inhibit reaching one's full potential.

According to Geoff Colvin in the book, *Talent is Overrated*, most managers believe that real success in business will always be created by the talented few.[14] Wrong! No business or school is successful if it is focused only on those who are "talented." It may appear that teachers are doing a great job when one-third of the children in their classrooms are achieving above grade level while others are struggling.

It does not surprise us that the potential of our own children is often described in measurement terms that imply there is a limit for each of them achieving success. In each case, with employees, students, or our own children, the potential to achieve is limited mostly by our own failure to arrange conditions that help them thrive.

Remember Jordi and her skills in teaching Junior to read (introduced in Chapter 1). She placed no limits on what she believed could be done if there was a positive change in his environment and the systematic use of positive consequences to teach him. Using her perspective when you look at behavior around you, you will find that it is not what people have done that defines what can be done, but what happens to shape and support next steps, progress toward the goal, today and in the future. Benjamin Franklin was onto something when he stated, "Carve mistakes in sand and successes in stone."

Competence Capped?

As described in his book, *Human Competence: Engineering Worthy Performance*, Thomas Gilbert created a simple way to measure improvement potential for any given workplace or other environment.[15] He used what he called a Performance Improvement Potential (PIP). It requires that you divide the top performer's accomplishments ("performance exemplar") by the average performer's accomplishments, to get a ratio of improvement. If the top performer is measured, for example, at 200 orders completed per hour, and the average production is 150 per hour, the (PIP) of that work team based on current machinery and processes, is 33 percent (200÷150=1.3333). An increase of over 30 percent in any business has a huge economic impact. Capturing such an improvement through these methods costs the organization very little. In addition, if done correctly, the initiative has an additional benefit of increasing the morale of those making the improvement.

Gilbert calculated PIPs for a variety of occupations, material that would be valuable for leaders in those industries to read and understand.

Bringing everyone who is below average up to average performance produces significant improvement before even setting the goal of getting everyone to the exemplar (highest) level. Very few companies are able to capture that level of potential, primarily because they typically focus on the lowest performers and use negative reinforcement as the main motivational tactic for improvement: "If you don't do better we will have to fire you." Helping people make marked improvements always produces surprises in uncovering those assumed to be marginal performers in the past but now are meeting the group average or exceeding it. We have seen this repeatedly.

The interesting thing about Dr. Gilbert's work is that he proved that the tremendous gains made by the individuals were made possible by arranging the conditions to reinforce the right behaviors by the individual. Peak performance for even the top performer could in fact be limited by the biases and conditions of the workplace, including the presence or absence of 1) a belief that even the highest and poorest performers could make improvements, thus shaping performance above current levels of performance, and 2) the rate and quality of reinforcement delivered to increase behavior. Gilbert never assumed that individual employees were smarter than others. He simply assumed a different history of reinforcement produced by the same environment, often dictated by assumptions of managers and others about the limits of individual performers. Gilbert knew that this could be changed.

Arranging Conditions for Individual Success

Those who learn how to shape well find that it is so naturally reinforcing that they are driven to do it even better. They seek to create situations where reinforcement is rapid and timely. A case in point, Morningside Academy, a private school in Seattle, Washington, has for the last 30 years increased learning by two or three grades a year per student.[16] These are average students who for a variety of reasons fell behind in school and had difficulty with particular subjects.

After being placed in a well-planned, behaviorally-based educational environment using individualized shaping strategies, the children have thrived and excelled. The staff finds the work in an environment that assumes children's potential as previously untapped, is highly reinforcing as well. The students report new social and academic achievements beyond what they imagined when they began. On a recent visit to the school, a former student told us how he thought he was "stupid" until he attended Morningside. Now in college, he had returned to Morningside to see if he could help students during his spring break.

In the typical school, structure, not function, dictates what schools, administrators, and teachers can do. However, the class or grade assigned should not be the determining factor for grade placement. In typical schools, teachers are often required to teach to a certain grade level, not skip ahead. Their methods assume a progression based on age and grade level, and if the third grade teacher were to teach fifth grade reading to her group, what would the fourth and fifth grade teachers do? The systems, processes, and assumptions of what defines a good academic environment all too often limit what teachers can do and what their students achieve.

Teachers often seek teaching environments where they are encouraged to apply principles of behavior, particularly the astonishing power of positive reinforcement, as children strive to master new learning. They are eager to measure their own success by evaluating their students' individual progress at frequent intervals. If these options were built into the systems and processes of the typical school, there is little doubt that teachers would thrive, as would students.

In business, don't keep your employees on a capped salary; rather, pay them for performance if you want to get them really committed to doing more to help achieve the goals of the business. For a way to design a compensation system that brings out the best in employees, begin with the book, *The Sin of Wages* by Bill Abernathy, and read his other books on performance pay. He designed successful compensation systems on pay for performance and behavioral scorecards in many companies across America and his books provide details on how to build an exceptional company, with members participating to their full potential. Arrange it so that performers achieve better results returning more profit and help them participate in the rewards of such growth.

Many years ago, a man who owned a company that built gasoline filling stations prospered greatly. As he was moving toward retirement, he asked a consultant to come up with a way for his employees to earn more money. The plan was simple: If the employees could come up with a way to save money on expenses without sacrificing quality, they could share in half of the savings. The result was that not only did the employees increase their pay by a substantial amount, but the owner more than doubled his profit as well. He was also able to build more stations due to the efficiency and cost savings devised and implemented by the employees.

One of the lessons here is that when your reinforcers result in the success of other people, both parties win.

Behavior Goes Where Reinforcement Flows

We said earlier that no person ever fits any label or stereotype exactly. We have never met the "average person." While in many ways a person's behavior and actions may be adequately described as average, there are probably just as many reasons why that same person would not be considered average. It may be worth noting here that science is all about finding general principles that describe all people, albeit not the average person. Dr. Gilbert's work demonstrated that change lies in the external world. Behavior will go to where there is reinforcement, and almost all people can learn if given the opportunity to do so.

The notion that our behavior is shaped by consequences is not new. What that implies about managing behavior is not fully understood in many settings. The answer lies in arranging conditions (the conditions that precede and follow behavior, antecedent, and consequences) to set up and support behavior to find its own way toward things (reinforcement) that helps to accelerate success for the individual, instead of having to control and manage every person's behavior or choices.

This science says in so many words, "Arrange conditions and get out of the way." To set up the best conditions for everyone winning, the next chapter looks at one more principle of the science of behavior that is fundamental to its effectiveness. The ABC Model has the capacity to address everything contained in the big wide world that surrounds behavior. It is often misunderstood.

8

The Two Ways to Change Behavior

There are only two ways to change behavior. You can do something *before the behavior* that you want to achieve to get it started, or you can do something *after the behavior has occurred* to keep it going. The technical term for what occurs before the behavior is *antecedent*. The technical term for what follows behavior is *consequence*. The two put together with behavior in the middle is shortened to the ABC Model. While it is easy to understand on the surface, the difficulty is in using it correctly and understanding how it accounts for all of what influences and maintains behavior (e.g., emotions, behavioral history, knowledge, meaning, effects, and actions). This model greatly informs us about how to initiate and sustain change.

In the Five-Step Model, when you identify ("pinpoint") the behavior to be changed, you are well on the way. Once you are satisfied that you have the behavior pinpointed, you can start the behavior-change process. The ABC Model has been used to successfully change millions of behaviors (no exaggeration). Even if you've never heard of it, any time behavior changes, it changes according to the scientific laws of behavior embedded in this simple model.

The antecedents that come before behavior are important—instructions, training, rules, signs, earnest pleas, emotional expression, warm requests—but never assume that these antecedents preceding behavior will assure that the behavior will occur. No matter how noble or intense the signal, it is the *consequence* of behavior that lends relevance to signs, pleas, and noble callings. Does the behavior occur? Does it occur again? The answers to those questions are determined by consequences.

Antecedents

According to the *Oxford Dictionary*, an *antecedent* is "a thing or event that existed before or logically precedes another." This is also a suitable description of the behavioral use of the term regarding placement in the ABC Model. An antecedent, by definition, always comes before the behavior of interest. However, the behavioral use of antecedents also includes information associated with the consequences of the behavior, the "C" of the ABC Model. If an antecedent has been associated with negative consequences produced by a certain behavior in the past, it is unlikely that it will prompt that behavior again. If it has been associated with positive consequences in the past, it is likely to prompt the behavior again.

Common words that are similar to the behavioral antecedent are *trigger, cue, prompt* and *stimulus*. They are often things that impact the senses, that is, things that you see, hear, touch, taste, or smell. Antecedents do their job when they point you toward an action. If you are hungry on a trip and you see a road sign for a favorite fast-food restaurant, it is likely that you will stop. But having just eaten, a sign for another favorite restaurant down the road will probably not cause you to stop and eat (see also Michael, 1982, 1993).[17]

Antecedents don't change behavior; they just get you in a position to experience a consequence of behavior that *will* change it. There is much more to learn about antecedents. Behavioral scientist Murray Sidman spent a significant part of his career researching just how they work.[18] The most common mistake in all aspects of our society is in the power that people assign to antecedents alone as a way to change behavior. People tend to believe that they can talk or instruct people into changing behavior.

We talk of inspiring, motivating, and energizing others by the words we use and the way we say them. However, if you are talked into making a change, it will only be temporary if the behavior does not also receive the right consequences to support it. No matter how strong the intent or desire to change has become, it will not be sufficient to produce a lasting change in the behavior if it does not result in some short-term benefit to the person changing, and at least some intermittent benefit to keep it going. Desire is not enough. How many times have you heard, or even said, "If you just make up your mind, you can do it!"

A sports broadcaster may say, "He just wanted it more than the other guy." What a useless explanation of why one player was more successful than the other one! Coach Bobby Dodd of Georgia Tech once asked "Bear" Bryant, the legendary football coach at the University of Alabama, what he did in the locker room to motivate his players before a game. Bryant's response was, "Nothing. If I have not done the job in preparing my players for the game by that time, there is nothing I can say that will make any difference."

Organizations, including government, waste billions of dollars trying new ways to communicate, motivate, engage, and involve people in some process or another when a final analysis shows that it was all talk (very expensive talk).

After all the talk, nothing has been done to change the consequences of people's actions; therefore, the behavior will remain exactly the same. In the 1980s and 1990s when the concept of "quality" was the rage in business, a manager stated, "All that has changed around here is the way we talk about quality."

If antecedents changed behavior, all that would be necessary to get compliance at home and work would be to communicate what needed to be done, and it would be done. We could have our children read a book on the importance of manners in a civil society and they would then demonstrate perfect manners at home and in public. We could read a book on golf and be expert golfers as a result. As we all know, that is not the case.

The most effective antecedents are the ones that most reliably predict a consequence. The ringing of a cell phone is an effective antecedent for the behavior of looking to see who is calling. It may not be an effective antecedent for answering the phone as you may not want to talk to the person calling. The sight of a speed limit sign may not be an antecedent to slow down, as the behavior of exceeding the speed limit is seldom followed by a speeding ticket. However, seeing a police officer nearby changes things and makes the antecedent more predictive of a ticket for speeding, thus resulting in drivers obeying the speed limit. These are clear instances of the ABC Model—the interaction of As and Cs to affect Bs.

Certainly, you can work on making antecedents more meaningful by demonstrating their direct relationship to consequences. In some classrooms, homes, and businesses the link between the two is an almost perfect match. Do this and this will happen. The more predictable the link between antecedent and consequence, the likelier it will be that the antecedent will be effective in prompting the behavior.

Consequences

As mentioned in Chapter 1 and it bears repeating here, the closest thing there is to a behavioral law is *behavior is a function of its consequences*. Antecedents alone don't cause sustained behavior change, but consequences do. To understand any behavior, look at its consequences. (This may call for a PIC/NIC Analysis®.) Consequences to strengthen individual behavior must be promptly connected to the response and delivered in ways that are reinforcing or punishing for the individual.

Without the close link between consequences and individual behavior there would be no real prediction and control over future actions. While control often is interpreted as "being controlled" or forced to do things against our wishes, its meaning really boils down to understanding the variables that determine our behavior, doing and saying things that work to achieve our goals. When we understand variables of behavioral control, we can use them to our advantage or toward helping others to produce desired outcomes.

In her book, *The Science of Consequences*, Susan Schneider shows how all animals, from the lowly flatworm to humans, learn from the consequences of their behavior.[19] Through interactions with our environment we learn to be competent, creative, confident, secure, insecure, shy, extroverted, combative, cooperative, et cetera. While many people think that some of those characterizations have a genetic origin, behavioral interventions show that even genetic predispositions can be modified, minimized, or eliminated by interactions with one's environment. Most people underestimate the role the environment plays in shaping our behavior, regardless of genetic factors. Achieving behavior change is often no more complex than changing the environment in deliberate and systematic ways.

The reason people think antecedents work is that sometimes they *appear* to work. If your mother called you to dinner, you eventually came, although it may have taken three or more calls to get the behavior she wanted. However, when you eventually responded, your mother was provided with intermittent positive reinforcement (consequence) for continuing to call you (antecedent). That is why this kind of behavior pattern is so hard for parents to stop. Yelling gets results. After several requests, what caused you to respond to your mother was the potential for the consequence to become more unpleasant.

When Mom raised her voice in anger, your experience with that tone of voice was a rather predictable negative consequence. Intermittent reinforcement produces strong habits and controls much of our behavior. The parents' behavior of yelling is strengthened even as they complain about having to yell to get results. If Mom calls again, although she said she wouldn't, her words eventually have little value in predicting her future action. She increases her yelling to a point that you have learned is the "tone of no return," and finally, you respond. Both are controlled by consequences; she by the effect the final, urgent tone produces and you by the potential consequence you know to be behind that tone.

In life, such escalation between parents and their children can lead to angry responses that can become very serious. This is clearly a lack of skill by the parent in observing behavior and taking positive actions to redirect unwanted behavior patterns in the first place. Raising one's voice is not terrible and almost everyone does it now and then, but using punishment to control future behavior, the consequences for not coming in the first place, can lead parents to increase the highly reinforcing strategies of punishment to control even mild disobedience. Instead, they should address the initial condition through more effective antecedents that include *describing* clearly what is needed and arranging PICs for *doing* what is needed.

It is a sad fact that most people convicted of committing a crime, after leaving prison, return to the same environment that shaped and maintained their criminal behavior. In such situations, odds favor more criminal behavior. While it may seem more complicated than that to those not acquainted with the laws of behavior, it really is that simple. It is not simplistic nor necessarily easy, but simple, clear, and easy to understand. However, simple answers are rejected by those who have tried unsuccessfully to change behavior for many years.

Because parents, executives, and government officials have tried many things in the past that have been unsuccessful, they usually arrive at the conclusion that complex problems require complex and often costly solutions. In the case of prisoners, many officials in the system have concluded that prisoners cannot be rehabilitated as they have witnessed prisoners go in and out of prison with a revolving door. The best and most reliable way to change such behavior is to create an environment that supports different (lawful) behavior. Sam Jenkins, a retired manager at International Paper, stated the problem in business accurately: "Managers consistently refuse to accept simple answers to complex problems."

Every behavior has a consequence that affects its future probability. Put more simply, people do what they do because of what happens to them when they do it. Those actions that we engage in are commonly referred to as *motivated*. People (and animals) are affected by the consequences that follow their actions to either repeat the activity, or to gradually or suddenly stop doing the activity. As a result of what we do, the consequences we experience cause us to either do a thing more or less in the future. Technically stated, positive and negative reinforcement increase the probability that we will repeat a behavior. Punishment and penalty decrease it. How much simpler can it be? Reinforce behavior that you want more of and punish or penalize behavior that you don't want.

It is important to use positive reinforcement more and to use punishment, threat, and fear infrequently, if at all. However, remember the parent who was yelling more? That yelling can escalate quickly into more negative behavior because the parent is getting reinforced through the use of threat and fear to control the behavior of the child. Sad and dangerous patterns can easily escalate into child abuse. Behaviors such as slapping and hitting the child for failure to respond can be justified by using a label to describe the child as hateful, disobedient, etc.

The only way people will ever reach their potential is through the effective use of positive reinforcement. Still, a significant number of adults have a belief in the moral correctness and strongly reinforced habits of using punishing consequences to get compliance, which is another way of saying that their use of punishment has been positively reinforced.

Although punishment sometimes gets compliance, it never gets the full realization of what an individual can do without the ever-present fear of the person using punishment. If you know of someone who yells and hits to get compliance from her children that does not mean she is getting anywhere near what could be achieved. However, it gives her an outcome she desires, and may look very good indeed to others, so it is highly likely she will yell or hit again. Brutal behavior is so often justified for the immediacy of the effects it gets.

You may have seen a program called *Child Genius* on television and wondered about the extremes of threat and fear some parents used and justified. Although they achieved a great deal with their children, one was left to wonder what else they could have done with greater positive support.

There is an old saying that fits this situation: "Change a person against her will, she's of the same opinion still." The next chapter will help you understand why this is the case and describe in greater detail that the effects of punishment on individuals and the larger society go well beyond simply getting one's way.

Study the four consequences shown in the figure below. All are useful. Three impact the performer negatively. However, the most efficient use of antecedents is to elicit a behavior that can be positively reinforced. Punishment and penalty stop behavior. Because some behavior will take its place, positive reinforcement should be used to strengthen the desired alternative. Even though negative reinforcement increases behavior, the fact that it gets just enough behavior to escape or avoid punishment limits what can be accomplished through its use.

Positive reinforcement leads to the acquisition of new information and skills without the negative side effects that come when punishment, threats, or fear are used to achieve the same behavior change.

Behavioral Consequences Model

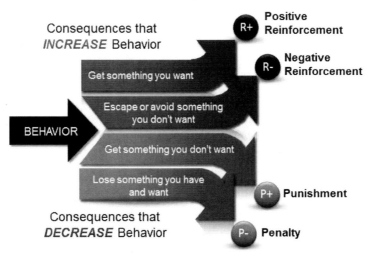

The side effects often reduce the focus on learning and positive change. The parent or boss using negative strategies often find that the recipients of those strategies will avoid that parent or boss whenever possible.

Strengthening behaviors you want rather than punishing those you don't want is a much more pleasant and productive way to spend your time. In addition, it is also more enjoyable and more exciting to those who are learning to change. One might say that establishing conditions of positive reinforcement is the most powerful method of managing yourself and others. Because positive reinforcement is so powerful, it must be used carefully or undesirable behaviors can be inadvertently strengthened. Most of us have been cautioned to watch for unintended consequences. If you reinforce the wrong behaviors, you are bound to get more of them.

Consequences designed to accelerate behavior through positive reinforcement need to be designed intentionally. Always consider the specific behavior that is being rein-forced. Some of the most destructive behavior patterns are produced by positive reinforcement. Gang behavior, lawless-ness, bullying, unsafe behavior at work; all may be positively reinforced even by actions that were applied to reduce them. We believe that most of the world's problems can be solved effectively by the *proper* use of positive consequences.

Everyone receives thousands of positive reinforcers every day. Behaviors (good and bad) are being strengthened every day. If you don't understand how this is happening, you are at the mercy of an ever-changing environment. If you understand it, you can take deliberate action to alter the environment in ways that are to the ultimate benefit of all.

Reinforcement is any consequence that *increases* the frequency of a behavior. Events can be positively reinforcing and lead to accelerated positive performance or they can be negatively reinforcing and lead to compliance or escape to avoid punishment. Parents think that sending a child to his room or putting him in time-out are punishers. Not necessarily. Is candy a positive reinforcer to a child? Not always. Is telling someone that she is doing a good job a positive reinforcer? Don't always count on it.

To know whether something is a reinforcer, we must first observe its effects on the behavior. Did the "punished" behavior stop? Did the "reinforced" behavior increase? We need to look at the behavior that occurs *after* the consequence has been delivered to know whether that particular consequence had an effect.

Positive reinforcement is so effective that it will strengthen the behavior that immediately precedes it (think PIC). If, however, done at the wrong time, for the wrong behavior, and in the wrong frequency, positive reinforcement can cause more problems than it solves. If that behavior is what the community values, the person will, if the consequence continues, be a more-valuable citizen. When the behavior that precedes positive reinforcement is not valued by society; for example, criminal behavior, and if the perpetrator is not caught and gets away with valuables, his criminal behavior of stealing will increase as well.

Positive reinforcement doesn't discriminate; its only effect is to strengthen behavior. Parents, business managers, and politicians can all strengthen the wrong behaviors. Even though their intentions are good, they may deliver a positive consequence at the wrong time (often delayed), therefore inadvertently reinforcing behaviors that produce undesirable outcomes. Negative consequences can be, and often are, positive consequences to the offender.

Why would terrorist organizations claim responsibility for a bombing that killed innocent civilians, including old people and children? Clearly, getting the word out through media reports of their heinous offenses offers positive reinforcement to the bombers. Their goals to eliminate anyone they believe doesn't have the right to live in their self-described ideal state are reinforced, increasing the likelihood of more deaths of the innocent. The communications also entice more recruits to their cause.

In this battle with terrorism, there will be many unintended consequences for society doing what we normally do, such as media reporting on the events. There may be positive consequences for terrorists from media attention, but many other consequences can be arranged to reduce their power, including how the media responds. Solutions to reduce the reinforcing properties of terrorist acts require complex responses across multiple areas of our public and private discourse. Even so, it is all about behavior and its consequence history. Knowing about the consequences that maintain this behavior, how it came to be and how it continues, is central to the solution.

Just the Facts on Positive Reinforcement

Detailed accounts of the power of reinforcement can be found throughout this book. However, several facts will help you apply positive reinforcement productively.

- *Positive reinforcement occurs when it is delivered after a behavior and increases the frequency of that behavior in the future.* By this definition, a frown, yelling, and screaming are reinforcers if they increase the behavior. If your child is becoming more rebellious, you can bet that the behaviors that you call rebellious are getting positive reinforcement from somewhere, possibly from you.
- *Positive reinforcers are highly individualistic.* Anything that is a positive reinforcer to one person may be a punisher to another. If someone made a list of their reinforcers, some things on that person's list

might appear on the list of many others, but some may not. It is only through observation that you can know if what a person *says* is reinforcing really does affect their behavior.

- *Immediate positive reinforcement is most effective.* Reinforcement begins to lose its effectiveness within minutes, sometimes within seconds, after the behavior has occurred. Think PIC.

- *One reinforcer doesn't change behavior much.* It takes many reinforcers (would you believe hundreds or thousands?) to establish a habit.

- *Positive reinforcers do not require the presence of another person.* For most people, making progress is a positive reinforcer. All computer games are designed so that the player can see progress. The average gamer may receive as many as one to two hundred positive reinforcers *per minute*! Completing tasks is almost always reinforcing. Any accomplishment, no matter how small, is positively reinforcing to almost everyone. Social reinforcers are important for those occasions where the natural consequences of a task do not provide reinforcers and in the right frequency to generate and sustain new behaviors.

- *Positive reinforcement accelerates and sustains behavior change while increasing satisfaction and confidence of the performer, through increasing mastery over the environment*

As you learn more about behavior and its consequences, link your antecedents reliably to clear and predictable consequences. Such deliberate antecedent management helps you set up positive conditions for change and begin to manage deliberately designed consequences to better ensure the change you want.

Consider the immediate and longer-term effects on the outcomes you want. As described above, you can arrange conditions to accelerate positive and immediate effects as well as help an individual achieve longer-lasting personal benefit. But first, nature seems to have arranged a bit of a barrier to getting this positive reinforcement stuff right.

9
Nature's Dirty Trick

One of the things that make it difficult to understand behavioral consequences is that sometimes their effects on behavior may not be immediately visible. For this reason, people often think that momentary consequences have no effect. That may mean that they cannot see change occurring when they deliberately follow a behavior with what they *perceive* as a behavioral consequence. However, behavioral consequences *always* change behavior.

The problem is that a single consequence usually changes behavior in a very small way, most of the time so small that people aren't able to see the change. This lack of immediate, visible effect leads many to say that consequences don't work on some people. That is a big misunderstanding. The only time something is a behavioral consequence is when it has an effect on behavior. It is defined by that effect, not by what someone thinks should be a consequence.

Sometimes we think we are selecting and deliberately using a consequence on a behavior when we are not. For example, "If you don't clean up your room, you are not going to like the consequence," is not a consequence. The consequence occurs when the child doesn't clean up his room and, as the parent stated, something actually happens that the child doesn't like. A threat is an antecedent. Following through with what was said is the consequence.

As we have said, immediate consequences are considerably more effective in changing behavior than those that are future or uncertain. Most of the things in life that cause us a lot of trouble are the things that give us immediate pleasure but long-term headaches and heartaches. Think of food, alcohol, drugs, and sex and their potentially addictive qualities. All of these activities can cause personal and societal problems.

Everyone who overindulges vows to change tomorrow, but most don't because the immediate consequences of indulging (in food, for example) are more powerful than the future, long-term negative consequences (gaining weight, etc.). For some, physiological addiction enters the picture as well, making the change all the harder. Even though people experience long-term negative consequences from their behavior, subsequent vows, intent, and determination to change (antecedents) often fail to override the immediate, positive consequences of their troublesome behavior. We have been asked many times, "If positive reinforcement is so effective, why does the default mode throughout the world seem to be to punish, penalize, or use negative reinforcement?" The reason is that nature pulls a dirty trick on us.

Nature's dirty trick is that punishment and coercion (negative reinforcement, using consequences based on threat and fear) are much more likely to produce an immediate consequence for the user than positive reinforcement, even though positive reinforcement is more likely to produce more desired behavior at higher rates without the negative side effects of punishment and coercion. Think back to the mother who yells and hits to get compliance quickly. Very often people are positively reinforced for using punishment more readily than they are for using positive reinforcement. Why is this?

Charles Darwin, originator of the theory of evolution through natural selection, showed that behavior that contributes to the survival of the species needs to be strengthened or else the species will not survive.[20] Therefore immediate, negative consequences perform an important function in survival by stopping dangerous behavior and reinforcing behavior that will facilitate escape or avoidance behaviors. This worked in primitive societies where survival was a daily concern, and it still works that way today. However, it also works on behavior that one could argue has nothing to do with the survival of the species. In fact, some might argue using punishment as a strategy may well lead to the disintegration of much of what we value in social interaction. It certainly can lead to diminished accomplishments and independent problem solving.

Think of it this way. For the caveman, running from an animal that would eat him was more important to his immediate survival than the potential of the positive reinforcement provided by killing the animal for food. Although physical survival is not a daily worry of most people today, consequences still work the same now as they worked from the beginning of time. In the story of the Garden of Eden, Eve faced the dilemma of immediate versus delayed consequences. Satisfying her curiosity and the sweet taste of the apple were positive and immediate, whereas the ultimate effects of eating the apple (and satisfying her curiosity) were negative, future, and uncertain (NFU).

Therefore, it is today that punishment is more likely to be used to change annoying or unwanted behavior than positive reinforcement. Punishment almost always provides the one doing the punishing with an immediate reinforcer (a PIC), because the person receiving the punishment reacts in a way that favors the goals of the punisher. The person receiving the punishment usually stops the undesired behavior or reacts in a way that lets you know they heard or understand your intent.

If you yell loudly at a child to stop what he is doing, he usually stops immediately, at least for the moment. If you yell at someone at work, the person will probably say or do something that lets you know that the consequence had an immediate impact. Yelling often does not work for long, but more severe punishment does, and thus nature's dirty trick takes on additional power and greater harm. Often it's easier to punish unwanted behavior than to positively reinforce a positive alternative. It takes less time and it gets a quick, visible response.

On the other hand, if you pat children on the head or give them a treat for helping you in some way, you do not necessarily see an immediate change in their behavior. If in the office you interrupt someone's work to tell her that she is doing a great job, you do not see an immediate change in her productivity. In both of these cases, you need to wait a period of time to evaluate the effects of your attempted reinforcement by what the person says and does. Ironically, in this way, nature tends to positively reinforce the use of punishment by its immediate effects, and fails to do the same for positive reinforcement.

The Abundance of Abusive Behavior

Because punishment is so very immediate, certain, and positive (PICs) for the punisher, producing the result desired in almost every case, the person punishing is very likely to use it again, finding it a quick and easy way to get compliance from those who do not do the things they want: spouses, children, workers, their peers, or anyone. That large effect by the one punishing in producing immediate and visible behavior change may be at the root of the *belief* that we are by nature aggressive.

Understanding how behavior gets established, even going back to the age of the caveman, and considering that behavior is a function of its consequences, the immediate effect of punishment on both the person punishing and the person being punished helps to more clearly explain why punishment, even its most extreme forms, occurs all too frequently and with such ease in today's society. Reinforcement is all too often not as dramatic and the changes desired are sometimes slow to start.

If a culture does not seek ways to use positive reinforcement to solve problems and enhance a civilized society, the default consequence will prevail and shape behavior toward an uncivilized state. The solution is to arrange the environment in such a way as to provide positive, immediate, certain consequences for behaviors that lead to a productive, creative, and peaceful life.

This solution may seem far removed from the lives of those who are brutal, abusive, and quick to anger and to those who are recipients of their actions. It may appear that only violence can end violence. Teaching children to make different choices is important and needs to begin as soon as possible when children first demonstrate a proclivity to hit or scream to get their way. It is equally important that adults quickly remove themselves and their children from situations where abusive behavior patterns (physical or verbal) are used to control others.

Just a little bit of tolerance reinforces the continuation of such behavior at high and steady rates. Instead of passive acceptance by those abused, such behavior requires a no-tolerance approach to changing the reinforcing properties of punishment, by immediately and consistently reinforcing alternative behaviors in children. It is especially important to change this highly reinforcing (addictive) pattern for the abuser, but first and foremost is getting the children away from the adult abuser. Highly reinforced, excessive force can rarely be changed in the settings that trigger such patterns. Safe harbor is needed at times as well. It is not an easy task. Ask any teacher who has a child demonstrating very aggressive behavior toward his peers. Ask an abused husband or wife.

Abuse is perhaps the single most difficult pattern to change. It is established through one's history of solving problems and the PICs offering the immediate effects of controlling the environment. It is one of the most pressing needs to address in our society today. However, aggressive patterns of behavior are not an unavoidable and predetermined part of human nature. It is not about raging hormones or our ancient histories as mammals on earth striving to survive. Rather, such behavior is shaped by the consequences that follow it. The degree of control the abuser has rests in the conditions that cultures promote and reinforce, including the cultures of families and communities.

Misunderstanding Punishment and Reinforcement Through Public Policy and Parental Practice

Fortunately, the number of people who understand that positive solutions are the only permanent way to educate people, manage a business, and live a happy, productive life, are increasing daily. They have been fortunate to have people in their lives who taught them the joy that comes from helping others succeed. However, because experience cannot be counted on to teach parents, business owners, and government and civic leaders how to do this in the most effective way, we still have people who promote laws, customs, and behaviors that they believe are consistent with a more positive society, but actually accomplish the opposite.

Because punishment produces an immediate response, people don't generally have to be taught how to punish. But the effects of positive reinforcement often take time to be observed, so people often have to be taught how to do it. Therefore, many people live long lives without knowing the pleasure and happiness that can come only when positive reinforcement defines their home and work lives—and that of the larger culture. Those who punish do not often come in contact with the negative effects of their behavior until children, spouses, and friends avoid them or escape from their control, but that kind of effect can come a long time after the punishers have had a steady dose of PICs for using coercive techniques to get their way.

We are certainly not saying that one should never use punishment. In situations where behavior is dangerous, unhealthy, or unfair, the behavior needs to be stopped and stopped immediately. In a situation where unfair treatment of others provides positive reinforcement to the perpetrator, that behavior needs a negative consequence to make it stop. Someone who breaks in line when others have been waiting patiently gets the advantage of a shorter wait, a better seat, and more immediate service (PIC). Without any negative consequence for doing so, such behavior will continue.

We see examples daily where a misunderstanding of the effectiveness of positive consequences and punishment are turned into a law, policy, or interpersonal interaction but are not consistent with producing lasting, positive outcomes. Often pop psychologists and others advise parents and managers to "always be positive" regardless of the behavior that is occurring. As you know by now that is about the worst advice you can ever receive. Being positive following negative behavior is likely to reinforce and therefore produce more negative behavior.

Punishment is defined as a consequence that stops a behavior. Parents saying no or frowning can stop behavior.

Telling the child what you disapprove of in clear terms can stop behavior. In the era of "positive parenting," large numbers of parents think that in the interest of creating a positive environment for their children, they should be tolerant of a wide range of negative behaviors by the child. By ignoring bad manners, rude or selfish behavior, or excusing it by saying the child is young, tired, smart, or a million other conditions, you are teaching something altogether unwanted. Such parental behavior allows the child to escape the appropriate consequences of rude or selfish behavior and instead provides positive, immediate, and certain reinforcement (a PIC) for that behavior.

Ignoring a person's behavior without addressing how a wrong act affects or harms others does not produce new learning about their effect on the world, even though they are often aware that what they are saying and doing is wrong. It can often produce confusion about whether or not anyone is really looking, or whether anyone cares enough to redirect their actions. If repeated enough, this will create bad habits that may take much future effort to change. As we have explained, PICs are very effective in establishing high-and-steady rates of behavior, whether the behavior is judged to be good or bad. The by-products for producing unearned PICs is to strengthen bad behavior that escalates over time if the strategy of ignoring behavior continues.

However, negative consequences are not particularly helpful. Parents want to be able to predict what their teenage children will do at a party when they're not around. Employers want to know that employees are doing things that add to the value of the business, even when supervision and management are absent. These are instances of encouraging and expecting positive self-control. Negative consequences do not teach that kind of self-control. The undesirable effects of negative attempts at controlling the behavior of others are detailed in Murray Sidman's book, *Coercion and Its Fall-out.*[21]

From a values perspective, negative control, especially punishment, should be used rarely and only as long as needed to produce a behavior that can be positively reinforced. Even that is tricky, because of the residual negative feelings (physiological reactions and private thoughts) that negative control creates, and the sense of power it conveys to those who are accustomed to getting their way through the use of coercive strategies.

Poet Maya Angelou said it well, "I may forget what you said; I may forget what you did; but I will always remember how you made me feel." This is why the famous UCLA basketball coach John Wooden did not allow negative behaviors such as cursing, berating teammates and other demeaning actions during practice or games. He knew that the negative feelings that lingered interfered with teamwork. Negative thoughts and feelings linger for a long time. Another problem with negative control is that while it suppresses behavior in the presence of the perpetrator, more often than not the same undesired behavior is likely to resurface when the person using such strategies is no longer in range (when the cat's away, the mice will play).

Some parents are surprised at the behavior of their children when they go off to spring break, or college, or move out of the parents' house. When the parents receive a call from the police, the college dean's office, or from the dormitory counselor, they are shocked at what their child has done. They often say, "But he never did that at home." If this has ever happened to you, you are certainly not alone. Helping children learn to deal with choice in ways that involve evaluating the impact of a choice they make on themselves and others is a valuable skill. Parents can help children anticipate the impact of their behavior on the well-being of others by discussing possible outcomes and evaluating their choices against this kind of values-based criteria. Such a future-directed way of helping children address choice by considering its impact on others is a big part of how wisdom is defined and developed.

Many people are concerned with teaching the tactics of *self-management* to children at an early age. Self-management is a broad term that includes how children handle their emotional reactions to events (such as The Marshmallow Experiment) and what they can do to arrange the environment so that they make good choices for themselves and others.

Education specialist Vicci Tucci designed a system called the Competent Learner Model® in which a part of its application focuses on helping three-, four-, or five-year-old children describe how their actions impact others, encouraging them to think about the immediate impact on their friends and family as well as the larger impact on the community.[22] It is quite amazing to watch a kindergartener go through a thoughtful analysis of the effects of his behavior on others. The teachers use this model to help children talk about pressures and discuss options without harsh judgment, as they work to understand actions they can take to influence their environment without harming themselves or others.

The evidence shows that the more they are taught alternative actions for a given situation, the more likely they are to choose a solution that is inclusive of others. Considerable emphasis is placed on helping children describe longer-term effects that, in turn, help them make better decisions. Those longer-term consequences may take effect no later than lunchtime, that afternoon, or the next day. With greater maturity, the timeline lengthens. Dr. Francis Mechner's Paideia School, mentioned in an earlier chapter, also emphasizes learning such techniques of self-management, calling such effort a component of demonstrating wisdom.

Dr. Robert Eisenberger's work (see page 20) provides valuable information about helping children learn effective self-management techniques and how these critical patterns of behavior are often associated with successful adults who make wise choices about their lives. He provides strong evidence as to how persistence, optimism, and many of the attributes seen as most highly correlated with successful adulthood are shaped by an abundance of PICs[23] for choices made during their childhood.

Many values-based behaviors are maintained by negative reinforcement (behavior controlled by the fear of disappointing a parent or disappointing God). Most of us learn early that violating the values we espouse can have long-term negative effects, including feelings of shame after behaving in ways that someone we care about would find very wrong. This kind of "conscience-building" is a valuable component of seeing ourselves as part of the larger world. It helps us express empathy, walk in another's shoes, and develop insights about how shame makes us reassess and seek to change ineffective behavior patterns.

People generally feel ashamed and embarrassed when they disappoint others. That kind of self-awareness makes us all more alert to our common humanity and to our connection to others. Sociopaths violate and disregard the rights of others, and normally do not feel guilty when hurting other people. They do not feel shame in the classic sense of having wronged another. They are not who you want your children to be.

Although negative consequences, including punishment, are a fact of life, our families, workplaces, and societies are better served when positive solutions are employed to build good habits. If we start to employ positive-change strategies to small behaviors, we can often blunt an escalation of potentially troublesome behavior, rather than reacting in such a way that inadvertently causes our children, spouses, or friends to spin out of control due to inadvertent reinforcement. Out-of-control behavior has almost always been shaped over time from a series of small, and often trivial, behaviors. Learning to intervene early and measure the effect is important.

The knowledge of the science of behavior allows us to anticipate how important it is to a person's future happiness and success to apply the proper consequences to small behaviors. Remember that the effect of positive reinforcement may take some time to show up in highly visible, new patterns of behavior. While it can be difficult to do, consider the longer-term positive effects to society of embarking on a plan of change using positive reinforcement strategies. Just as the Competent Learner Model® does for children, positive strategies for addressing change have significant impact on everyone.

That said, the practice of giving every child a trophy regardless of what the child does cheapens the value of the trophies for the children who earned them. Give a trophy to everyone who attends every practice if you wish, because attending every practice is at least a behavioral requirement. However, think of positive reinforcement as something that is *earned*, not something that happens to you because you just happen to be in the right place at the right time.

Studies show that non-contingent (unearned) positive reinforcement actually degrades performance. Many seriously depressed teenagers report that they don't have to do anything at all to get all the material goods they want. Nothing is expected of them. Therefore, when they do things that are wrong or violate rules, they may be given a bigger television or the keys to the car after a short lecture or no lecture at all. They often describe the absence of negative consequences as feeling like the absence of caring. In the end, they report feeling that their behavior does not matter. When effort is not wanted or expected from them, they are at risk of feeling unwanted and unloved. Those who get too little positive reinforcement despite doing good things—making that A- instead of an A+, never hearing about what they did well but only what they need to do more of and better—also often show up depressed. Nothing they do is good enough. They are not good enough. They will only disappoint. They feel they are a burden.

Getting something intended to be positive for repeatedly doing the wrong things often leads to depression. Repeatedly getting nothing positive for good things you have done has the same effect. Additionally, by using reinforcement non-contingently, you rob the person of facing the meaning his actions have made in the world or the good feelings and satisfactions that come from real accomplishments. This does not mean, however, that you stand aside, waiting for failure or success while withholding reinforcement.

The most powerful tool you have to shape positive behavior is the meaningful application of positive reinforcement, when you see behavior trending in the right direction. The behavior doesn't have to be perfect or even near perfect, but it should be heading in the direction you want. Because positive reinforcement is so powerful in increasing new behavior, it needs to be done precisely at the right time and with the right frequency or you run the risk of inadvertently strengthening the wrong behavior. It matters little whether the "behaver" is a scientist doing research in a laboratory, a mother teaching a child to "behave," a diplomat working on a treaty between two warring rivals, or a business person striving to improve the profitability of her business; positive reinforcement works when valuable behaviors are pinpointed and effective consequences are delivered.

We hope that understanding nature's dirty trick will help you find ways to avoid using negative consequences and experiencing their costly, negative side effects. To better ensure you provide many more PICs than NICs in supporting the development of others, track what you say and do to encourage the change you want.

10

Making Change Transparent

A very important value in changing behavior is that whatever we do to others should be evaluated through some kind of measurement system. If you claim you can change behavior, be prepared to prove it. A criterion of scientific measurement is that the change can be replicated and supported in visible and measurable ways. Measurement and feedback, steps 2 and 3 of the Five-Step Model, provide the tools of validation.

It seems that every successful coach, athlete, retired CEO, and politician writes a book on either motivation or leadership. The source of their knowledge is most often just memories of their personal experiences that in many cases bear slight resemblance to what actually happened.

Most of the methods these books and lectures tout cannot be replicated. Still, people continue to buy these books and attend lectures hoping that they will glean a tidbit of information to help them deal more effectively with their friends, families, and co-workers. More often than not, they are disappointed when they try to apply what they read or heard to real-life problems. *Flavor of the Month* is a derisive phrase used for business-improvement programs. The reaction of most employees on hearing about the latest attempt to improve some aspect of business performance is, "Here we go again." These initiatives fail because the results that the new company expected are not produced, be it teamwork, safety first, customer excellence, and so on. Each requires clear pinpoints about desired results and necessary behaviors to address the issues, skill in coaching and shaping, and well-designed consequence systems to sustain effort.

For years, businesses have tried process and systems redesign to solve employee issues of low engagement, safety, productivity, customer service, and cost. They spend days or weeks revising mission, vision, and values statements, speaking of new commitments to empower employees, making improvements in benefits, restructuring management, and implementing programs such as Six Sigma and lean manufacturing, that promise much and deliver little. Such activities, summarized here as *engagement strategies*, are often promoted by various business gurus as sure ways to increase motivation. However, because the implementations violate one or more of the principles presented in this book, these investments in new initiatives become a waste of time and money.

All too often we excuse our own behavior based on superstitious interpretations of what causes the actions we take. You may remember the wonder of the Ouija board when you were young. As children, we watched in sheer amazement as our hands moved across the board, being pulled, we were sure, by some magical spirit force to land over the right letters and numbers that would help to predict our future. Most of us mastered the art of muscle resistance and pull very well during the game, whether or not we believed that magic forces were moving our hand. For all too many, however, the Ouija board and other forms of fortune telling remain. This chapter introduces another way of knowing that frees us from relying on superstition. It is a different way to understand and predict how to better influence behavior in the future.

Sometimes we want to believe something no matter what the evidence against it. We know that it must be true, and that if it isn't true, at least it provides hope to those who need it to be true. Almost anything that provides a persuasive presentation is comforting in the moment, but if it is in fact an illusion, in the end it offers only delay in getting to solutions that work.

Many people are helped by being promised what they call *hope*. When children cannot talk, walk, or read because of severe physical or behavioral issues, parents suffer too. They want to find treatment that makes a difference, and in seeking solutions they sometimes fall prey to charlatans, con artists, and scams. Of course, the child or person who engages in treatment that is not valid or reliable is not helped; yet many have embraced false methods for a variety of problems. In desperation, people seeking solutions will invest in and trust people who claim they can communicate with dead relatives, rainmakers during a drought, and preachers who promise relief from terrible pain, or invest in the palm-reading charlatan who predicts that love is right around the corner, *for a fee*.

It wasn't too many years ago when *Facilitated Communication* was presented as the wave of the future for teaching non-verbal children to communicate. Parents flocked to presentations and meetings to enroll their children who were non-verbal. Somewhat like the Ouija board, using this method, a facilitator passively holds the arm of a special needs student (for example, a student with an autism spectrum-disorder diagnosis who does not speak). The student will then supposedly indicate which key to press to type a message for the teacher or others. Many parents and teachers accepted the idea that communication could be facilitated by holding the non-communicative child's arm over a keypad as she types her wants and needs enthusi-astically.

However, in a large number of studies across multiple disciplines, the communication has been found to be ever-so-subtly directed by the facilitator, not adding at all to true communication skills, and judged to be pseudo-scientific. Despite that finding, this practice remains in vogue today with ardent supporters, no matter what the research has demonstrated.

The issue here is not the very understandable desires of parents to help their children communicate, but the destruction that occurs when society supports undocumented methods of treatment without demanding that they be subject to the rigors of scientific validation. Unexamined acceptance of such solutions only increases the time such children are delayed from participating in solutions that really could unlock their potential.

The health community worldwide has worked tirelessly to have vaccines accepted around the world. They have helped virtually eradicate such childhood scourges as rubella, whooping cough, measles, and polio, all of which killed and maimed children. In 2014, however, measles reentered America at an alarming rate, in part because of personal *beliefs* about the alleged harmful effects of vaccination supported by an article in *The Lancet,* a reputable medical journal. Subsequently, *The Lancet* withdrew the article and the primary author, Arthur Wakefield, was discredited by the medical association and fired from his medical position. Because scientists are modest in their certainty, it took several years for the article to be withdrawn and for the medical community to denounce his fraud.

Scientists caution that more needs to be studied and evaluated before absolutes can be stated about something as complex as causal relationships. Many in the public arena who make claims with certainty do not adopt this most critical element of the scientific method when reporting their beliefs.

Sorting the Wheat from the Chaff

Everyone believes things that they think they know, only to find out later that they are false. People believe many things with little to no proof, even though much evidence exists indicating that those beliefs are not true. In no other area of life is this truer than in matters of human behavior. In particular, belief about the causes and maintenance of human behavior is rarely subject to scrutiny beyond that of personal experiences. People often rely on personal experience, common sense, authority, close relationships, or successful people's testimony as the primary way of knowing, especially when science is difficult to understand or not known. The problem with these unscientific ways of knowing is that even when everyone agrees, it is possible that all of them are wrong.

How do we know that our current beliefs about the causes of our actions are true or not? Are there ways to get us beyond our own experience to sort out how best to change ourselves and others? One of your neighbors, friends, or family members will tell you about a remedy for your aches and pains and another will tell you the exact opposite. How do you know who is right, who to believe?

We learned years ago that facts don't sell. We don't often persuade or dissuade people with our tried and true facts. But people do promote sources that they trust or consider reliable. For example, if we believe that one of our friends is smarter than the other, we may likely follow his recommendations. There are numerous ways we gather advice about how to behave in certain relationships. New mothers will trust the pediatrician to give good advice about a wide range of subjects because she has given good advice as to the care of her baby. Because of this relationship, she may trust her opinions about other subjects outside of the medical field even though she may be wrong. This is certainly true when medical doctors give advice about behavior problems.

Everyone has their own facts, that is, their *interpretation* of the facts. Science is about applying a particular set of methods to collect and evaluate evidence, and about following certain rules when interpreting the findings. The words *systematic* and *replicable* best capture the methods and interpretations of science.

Democrats and Republicans, having the same data (facts), often support diametrically opposed solutions based on passionately held beliefs about what is best for all. In almost every criminal trial, both the defense and the prosecution have their own experts who, after reviewing the same data, come to opposite conclusions. Science provides a method for analyzing whether "facts" are reliable and predictable. It is called *replication*.

One day we hear on television that a scientific study has found that caffeine is bad for your health and the next day or month, we hear that another study has found it is good for you. Who do you believe? When you see a television ad that says nine out of 10 dentists recommend a certain brand of toothpaste, what does that mean? If our current toothpaste works fine, why go to the trouble? After all, our parents used the brand and they still have their teeth. Of course, making a decision about the brand of toothpaste we use is certainly trivial compared to decisions we make about relationships with others.

Decisions we make about people can have far-reaching effects. Decisions may be about how to respond to a child who is on drugs, a spouse who has been unfaithful, an employee who has been found to treat fellow employees poorly, and a thousand other interpersonal decisions that we all face over time. Decisions we make about ourselves and others turn out to be very important to personal happiness, financial and business success, and to the happiness of others with whom we interact. Indeed, the collective decisions that shape our cultural patterns of behavior as well as those of other nations have tremendous impact on the world we inhabit.

In today's world we have access to incredible amounts of information via Facebook, Twitter, Instagram, blogs, and other social media. As many have learned, passing something on to your friends that showed up on your computer all too often turns out to be fraudulent rather than factual. Not infrequently, one of your friends who received some information from you replies, requesting that you check it out with Snopes.com or some other website that debunks the information you sent. David and Barbara Mikkelson originated Snopes.com and are responsible for much of the research.[24] While they and their staff work hard at getting the facts right, they, too, are subject to bias and sometimes get it wrong. They are not, however, offering scientific proof, but rather, they are professional researchers and writers, uncovering facts about rumors.

Gathering the right facts surrounding an event or an assumption is not the same as applying the scientific method to analyze what we accept as fact. Sometimes we mistake the two—facts and science. Facts about events that occurred that may involve human behavior are not the same as describing an underlying scientific principle related to how or why that behavior occurred. A fact is just a fact and is not bound by the scientific method. "Facts" and scientific principles are different and it is important to understand that difference.

Science as a Guide

Good science requires replication. How many studies show the same result? In every case it is important to look at the data and see how the data were obtained. When evaluating a study it is important to understand what the scientists actually did and how they interpreted the data.

Almost all scientifically verified facts involve some interpretation. Interpretation introduces many possibilities for misinterpretation. Before you act on or pass information to your friends, look at the methods used to collect the data to determine the validity of the interpretations before the proponents of such data told others "the facts" about their study. Did the toothpaste study ask only 10 dentists? Did they ask 1,000? Did they ask many groups of 10 dentists until they found one group where nine out of the 10 recommended a certain brand? Did they pay the doctors for their opinion? Were the doctors aware of which toothpaste was the sponsor's toothpaste?

In any of these cases, the dentists were not necessarily lying, but people can be persuaded by the way information is presented. It is important to know these details to make a decision about data as presented and not automatically accept someone's interpretation of it. It is also important to know how the data were collected before you can reliably trust that the study was scientific in its methodology. You can even be tripped up with what appears to be simple facts.

During the Cold War there was a comical and most likely exaggerated story circulating about the results of an athletic competition between the United States and Russia. There were many such competitions between the U.S. and Russia in those days—space, athletics, geopolitical conversions, nuclear armament. While we don't know the race to which this story refers and we don't even know if it is true, it provides an excellent teaching point about data and the use of numbers. Although the U.S. won, and with only these two engaged in the race, the story in the old Soviet newspaper *Pravda* the following day supposedly read: "In the International Race yesterday, Russia came in second place; the United States came in next to last."

Most people would describe themselves as doing well in running their lives without considering scientific research. Yet, understanding why and how we do what we do can improve the decisions we make and allow us the opportunity to purposefully influence behavior in humane and meaningful directions. Behavioral principles are universal and are in play with all people, everywhere, all of the time. Understanding the principles is not necessary for many good colleagues, parents, teachers, caregivers, and leaders in business and society to do the right thing, but in many cases, a better understanding of those principles can help. And in some of those cases, it is essential.

Many individuals are working to uncover methods for how best to learn, to master our environments, to establish values that support doing the right thing as we know it, and to arrange conditions for our continuing success. Complex issues of culture and change across the larger society as well as specific data about how best to arrange conditions for change at the individual and group level are addressed through both basic and applied research. Each year the Association of Behavior Analysis International (ABAI) presents between 1,500 to 2,000 research papers at its annual conference and has been doing so for over 40 years.[25] Members write books and publish in refereed journals containing evidence-based studies about principles of behavior.

Demonstrating the generalizability of the science across cultures, researchers in countries around the world present their work on fundamental principles of learning. Through such work, it is clear that while cultural and individual practices may vary, the laws of behavior unite the human race.

Much has been learned, but even more remains unknown. The majority of the population has never heard of our particular scientific association (ABAI). Most people at home and at work make decisions about how to raise their children, maintain their marriages, and run their businesses based on opinions gathered from family, friends, and other non-scientific sources, as well as their own history of reinforcement—methods that they may have used to address human behavior when they were growing up. While that may work well, it may lead to patterns of behavior described in this book that do not work well and at times even cause harm.

It is important to understand causes of human behavior, not based on superstition, rumor, or even experience, but rather based on scientifically verified principles that you can count on to produce reliable and valid changes. Science is the best "myth buster" available.

The scientific method provides us with a way of knowing the truth, defined as objective, measurable, reliable, predictable, and repeatable. It assures you that you will achieve the same results over and over again. You then can say that what you have learned is *true*, as close to truth as one can get.

We know about behavior when we can predict and control it. The best way to "predict" what anyone will do is to observe what they do in similar circumstances. "Control" in the sense that we use it is about arranging conditions of positive consequences to increase the likelihood that a person selects one behavior over another.

The scientific method allows us to see how to shape worthwhile performance in ourselves and others in the present moment and measure progress along the way, even when the desired final effects can only be known sometime in the future. These small shifts toward positive behavior take hold quickly in most cases, allowing us to direct our behavior toward worthwhile outcomes. Measuring and graphing behavior are key to understanding if in fact we are affecting change with scientific precision. It can make the difference in helping someone have a life of meaning and success rather than a life of mistakes and negative behavior patterns.

Remember, however, despite how clean this sounds, the environment provides many sources of control over immediate behavior that have nothing to do with what we might carefully arrange to ensure particular behavior will happen. Our unique human histories are still interacting with a myriad of possible sources of reinforcement, shaping what we say and do.

Track the Change You Want

Thousands, if not millions, of people worldwide own some kind of tracking device. These trackers continuously monitor steps, heartbeat, weight, and so on. If you watch people who wear a Fitbit® step tracker, you will see them frequently checking to see how many steps they have taken. Seeing the data allows the person to see how much they have done, or not done, and how much they have to do to reach their daily goal. Seeing the number of steps taken is often a reinforcer if you have taken many steps, and an antecedent to do more if you have taken few steps. The trackers perform at least two functions. First, they provide positive reinforcement when you see improvement or high numbers, and second, they are an antecedent to do more when numbers are not where you want them to be.

We advise people to put the data on a graph so that they can see where they are at present, where they have been, and where they have to go. As you can imagine, for anyone who is tracking their performance, checking and plotting the data provides many reinforcers. On a long run, the runner checks many times to see how she is doing. Later, seeing the results of many such runs plotted on a graph provides many reinforcers that keep the person running. Both authors have experience with years of tracking behavior and its reinforcing properties for keeping desired behavior going, even when distractions might occasionally interfere.

Changes you take on need not start large. Remember, every step counts, one behavior at a time. Most change is in the day to day. Take the time to figure out the results you want. Return to the Five-Step Model. Pinpoint both the results and the behaviors needed to get there. Set small goals along the way. Then track what you do, increasing your child's confidence by catching her doing things right, not commenting when she makes a small mistake; mastering a requested skill at work to advance your position; becoming a friendlier person to increase more social contact outside of work; exercising more to feel healthier, and use the PIC/NIC Analysis® to figure out how to get more of what you want as you go forward.

If you want to be a friendlier person, track what you do and say to others to increase positive interactions. Begin where you are and recognize your effort by jotting it down. Whatever it is, you can pinpoint it and measure and track it. You can build in reinforcers and ask others to help you keep that behavior going by commenting on and recognizing your efforts, from high-fives to descriptions of the change they see. Tell your story of how you are changing to a special friend. That in itself can keep behavior going in the right direction.

Our experience shows that the simple act of tracking any behavior you want to change, putting the results on a graph so you and others can see trend lines and positively reinforcing progress toward that goal, solves many, many problems.

The methods provided here should help you start developing your own plans for behavior change. However, the process is not complete unless you consider that what you do may at times have unintended consequences, supporting or clashing with the interests and well-being of others and of our society.

The next and final chapter describes ways to develop greater sensitivity to increasing the connection between the intention to do the right thing and the effects that our behavior has on larger cultural values that can affect the whole world.

11

Creating a Better World

Now that you are more familiar with what behavior is and how to change it, consider the role of values in guiding what we say and do, including considerations about if and when it is appropriate to change another person's behavior.

We are part of a pluralistic society striving to balance diverse values that are important to our sense of right and justice. When you help another person change behavior, you often deal with everyday kinds of issues. Rarely will you deliberately connect your actions to making this a better world. We know it may seem a stretch to emphasize that using science-based principles of behavior change can make for a better world, but if your approach to change arises from a solid desire to increase good effects; we are confident that these principles can help.

Science does not tell us if our behavior is going to create a more ethical society. It makes no judgment about whether what we say or do is wise or foolish. Science does not supply us with a method to analyze whether our actions are for the greater good or not. However, understanding how behavior comes to be may create a more tolerant world that is less fixed on the notion that humans are limited by their histories, by flaws of personality, or other internal states. Behavior analysis helps us see the actions of others objectively, assess the effects of consequences, and determine the next steps for behavior change.

This science alone will not help us act with wisdom or in more ethical ways as determined by the rules of conduct in our society, nor will it help us act with greater morality, as each of us has learned to define our own personal code of conduct. However, working to arrange consequences for desired behavior that also promotes a values-driven life can help.

Creating a Values-Driven Life

By now, you have a better understanding of the power of reinforcement. Because behavior can be reinforced to do great good or great harm, it is important to work toward *good* for our children, families, communities, and culture. It is important as well to see beyond our immediate interests when possible. Values such as cooperation, kindness, persistence, and truth telling are what we would hope might be visible byproducts that are directly shaped when working with others. But without intending to do so, extortion, stealing, domination, coercion, and other harmful patterns of behavior can be inadvertently or directly reinforced.

Becoming more alert to the larger effects of behavior on the values we espouse is important for anyone who wants to increase effectiveness in changing behavior. Moving beyond examining whether behavior is ethical based on good intentions alone, to more fully evaluating its longer-term effects, is the cornerstone of our individual ethical and moral footprint.

We can most likely agree that it would be great if we could resolve the conditions we mentioned in Chapter 1: war, poverty, illiteracy, crime, prejudice, abuse, and other major problems of society. We know that rules of conduct most important to the future of humankind can be reinforced and shaped. You have only to look around to see that these science-based laws of behavior have created wise, patient, creative, innovative, and persistent adults, as well as impatient, rigid, and chaotic adults. This knowledge of how such varied patterns of behavior come to be can be used to help create and maintain a civilized society. When we look to those individuals who are exemplars in demonstrating the best of values, we know they got there through the effects of consequences for doing the right things in the right ways for the right reasons over time and in varying environments.

Behavior is changed every day in deliberate and unintentional ways, including by the reciprocal effects people have on one another. When you change in relation to me, I change. When I change, you change. The question that might come up is, "If that is so, am I changing your behavior in ways that benefit both of us, or am I changing your behavior in ways that benefits one of us to the detriment of the other?" Behavioral effects link us one to another. In that way we are our brothers' and sisters' keepers.

Many people, before they understood and applied this science, reported to us that they were actually influencing behavior at home, school, in places of worship, at work, and in the neighborhood, in ways that they did not understand or necessarily want to do, behaviors that they strengthened even as they complained about them.

As people learn to look, listen, respond, and evaluate, they find that they can take this knowledge of behavior to change their immediate world and that of others for the better. They learn to use the PIC/NIC Analysis® to figure out the consequences that are maintaining, suppressing, or accelerating behavior, and then they start to arrange conditions that produce the desired effects they want to see or do more of, such as *cooperation* or *acting with integrity*. They know to pinpoint behaviors that show up as cooperation or integrity and they are often very skillful in teaching others to identify what they need to do to demonstrate more cooperation or acting with integrity. They also know how to get such behavior to become habits, showing up across conditions with consistency and clarity—becoming how others see them, becoming "who the person is": a part of their character as judged by others.

Once these value words and phrases are pinpointed more precisely, many people seek to incorporate values they espouse through selective behavior change. Leaders may do more asking and listening than telling and demanding. Employees may express appreciation for the help of a colleague, and a student may provide useful ideas to someone who is having difficulty completing an assignment.

Some say that behavior analysis cannot help people get to the highest order of values because focusing on behavior is too mechanistic and too externally focused to really explain or bring out the best in all of us. Remember the woman who learned to go outside after staying inside for many years, and for 40 years afterwards called her therapist on his birthday to update him and thank him for helping her find a deeply satisfying life? Her change, because of the application of behavioral methods, was profound and lasting and led to a much more fulfilling life that had positive effects on her family and friends.

When great poets talk of loving another to the depth of their souls, they too are responding to what they see and hear another say and do. Creation is at its best when there are positive consequences for remaining engaged in creative behavior. This technology is not only a technology for simple change, but also for the most profound changes at a personal level, across society, and throughout cultures around the world. This science provides methods for each of us to behave in ways that can increase conditions to lead a rich and full life.

Got Values?

Nothing up to now about understanding behavior and its consequences will require that you define whether or not your actions are good or bad for our society as a whole. This science can provide you with excellent tools for developing new behavior (the tools of shaping) using positive control (a value you can adopt in refusing to use punishment as a primary method of creating change with others), and it can provide excellent tools for stopping behavior that impedes or harms others (correction and redirection), but it cannot tell you *per se* whether the behavior you are working to create is good or bad.

Only when you hold up your actions to society's lens do you know the messages your behavior sends to others about your values. Sometimes you may need to hold your actions up to values beyond the particular society in which you find yourself, measured against universal principles of what defines us as humans striving to increase the humanity of us all.

To create a society that is measured by its commitments to a common set of values, it is important to have agreement on what those values are. Whether we do the right thing is determined in the end not by what we *say* we do and what we *want* the effect to be, but by measuring the behaviors that we actually exhibit and how those behaviors affect the larger society.

Truth telling is represented by many behaviors over time, but even after decades of telling the truth, being labeled a liar can occur from a single instance. Because what we do is affected by consequences that occur in the moment, it is important when thinking about values to think about a person's efforts and effects over the longer term. These principles of behavior change are not morality measures, but rather they are objective ways to observe, measure, and change behavior to produce the results we want. When we speak about a person having a core set of values or displaying inappropriate values, those attributes are labels for what we see people say and do.

Because what is said and done can be changed, we need not wait for the values to change. Change behavior and the negative (and positive) values attached to particular behavior patterns change; that is, receive a different label: from liar to truth teller, for example.

Our values are shaped by behavioral consequences. Many times when people lie, it is because they know that if they tell the truth they (or someone they care about) will be punished. Sometimes it just works for them, gets them out of tough situations, or reinforces next steps by promotion to a better job. Nevertheless, principles of behavior can increase truth telling in tough situations and in obtaining promotions.

Applying the lessons of unintended consequences, we may on occasion negatively impact the very behavior we want. Lecturing and telling will never get us as strong a set of values as those values that develop when others behave in the desired ways because of appropriate consequences. When their behavior is linked to a core value and is celebrated, that is another way to strengthen a values-based decision process for saying and doing particular things. Comment on the good values that are represented by the actions of the person by describing specific behavior that represents, for you, integrity, respect, truth telling, and so on. Specific behavioral descriptions help to reinforce future actions that demonstrate those values.

Think about the kind of environment you create for those who are influenced by you. Do you reinforce actions you value in others? Do you let them know what you see them saying and doing that reflects their own modeling of wisdom in action? The qualities we often associate with high moral values are defined quite simply by actions and patterns of behavior persistently demonstrated over time and situations. Letting people know what you see from a values perspective is important and it is often highly reinforcing in maintaining such actions.

Values are names we give to behavior patterns that are, for us, representative of larger meaning. One value can refer to the same kinds of behavior that leads to another value-based name. If we want cooperation, for example, we can define that as "sharing with others, taking turns, following instructions, and contributing ideas to the group." These same behaviors can be described as demonstrating respect for others. Each of those behaviors can be seen or heard in our words and actions.

Values are defined by how they are seen as showing up in patterns of behavior. The more we consistently demonstrate behaviors that the group defines as reflective of cooperation, for example, the more we will be called cooperative. If we are uncooperative, we may need to "take turns, share with others, follow instructions, and contribute our ideas to the group." Sometimes, though, integrity requires that we take actions that differ from the actions desired by the majority. Those actions may require not cooperating with the group. Remember Robert who refused to agree in a meeting about production and failed to get his well-deserved promotion? He did what he knew to be the right thing.

No single behavior can determine whether or not you are living a values-driven life. Telling a lie when you know that by telling the truth you put someone in danger can be a demonstration of good values—protecting and caring for others.

When robbers come in pointing a gun, asking if anyone else is there, and you say no when in fact there is a baby sleeping in a bed, is an example of lying for a greater good or *doing no harm*. Context matters.

The longer-term effect of your actions, intended and unintended, are elements to evaluate how well you are doing in striving to live a positive, values-based life. It is a journey that is not character-driven but consequence-driven. This area is one where we can benefit from the reflection of others on the effects of our behavior if we are to ensure we are striving to be ethical. In many situations, the wrong decision is the one with the most PICs while the correct, positive, values-based decision often only has PFU consequences, with lots of immediate NICs.

When you start to measure the effects your actions actually have on others, you are attaching value to your action. Whether the actions are large or small, each decision you make when solving problems of human interaction can add or remove value to or from the larger principles that society teaches us about human action. Doing the right things, in the right way, for the right reasons, is often defined as ethical.

The vast majority of people caught up in ethical scandals are by no means intending to be unethical. They are not thieves by design, nor do they intend to have the word *criminal* show up on their carefully developed resumes. They often evaluate what they did when caught in an ethical misstep or even a deep dive into bad deeds as, *intending* to be ethical. That is, doing what is good for the team, meets their manager's requirements, or fulfils the mission of their "great place to work" company so the business can remain open. These are all examples of doing the right thing, as *right* is understood in certain conditions. However, when unethical conduct occurs, the individual is still held to be responsible by the larger society, whether particular actions are intentionally unethical or not.

The lesson is that in the workplace, the community, or at home, character alone is not enough. Slipping down a slippery slope toward unethical behavior is all too easy. PICs and NICs demonstrate the control that is exercised by consequences in the moment. Arranging PICs for actions involving the achievement of an effect that may delay a much desired reinforcer can help in striving to be ethical. Avoiding NICs, something we all want to do, can cause a person to do the wrong thing, even when knowing it is wrong. Thus living a life where a significant part of what we do is assessed against how we demonstrate core values over time is difficult, and every day is Groundhog Day. Each and every day, we might have to begin over to see if our actions are having and will continue to have the right effect.

We often *say* what we believe to be the right things, but when observed, we often are more likely to *do* what is reinforcing for us. The research on this *say/do* correlation generally indicates a weak bond between words (say) and actions (do). The two do not always match and many people are unaware of this disconnect. Wanting to do right and talking in those terms is very important, but it is not enough.

Whether an act is ethical or not can sometimes be immediately defined, as in cases of flagrant fraud or misdeed, but for many behaviors, we can only see in retrospect how those behaviors eventually affected the larger group. Good intentions today can lead someone right to jail later, such as failing to report a friend for what might be considered a minor safety violation in leaving the job early. She may have had a sick child and she does not do such things frequently. That violation may be part of a pattern, however, that leads to what may later be judged to be an unethical act by being away from her post during a crisis.

Turning ourselves into ethics police is not helpful either. It can be nuanced and unclear whether there is an ethical issue in a choice that is made. It requires care in whether or not a judgment is made about something that could be handled by skill training, or discussion of alterative choices, or by reporting an individual for something that was of little significance and unlikely to ever happened again.

All of us behave, as we have seen, along a continuum of reinforcement for what we say and do. Evaluating whether or not something someone does is truly unethical (or rather a bad choice), is difficult. No one wants to get into situational ethics, evaluating the effects by whether or not, for example, anyone is likely to get caught.

Often the truth of whether an action is unethical or a faulty (but repairable) decision cannot be made until sometime in the future. This lagging definition makes for what constitutes ethical conduct a difficult topic at times. Such delay can seem far removed from individual accountability, and rarely do companies or families do a thorough analysis to assess how consequences could have indicated such an outcome, discovering the behaviors that led to the misdeeds that befall them (think of Bernie Madoff's family and Enron's leadership team).

Many companies are establishing ethical analysis processes by which to evaluate the near-term and longer-term effects of actions, even as they are occurring. They help assess the ethical impact of actions through such tools as the PIC\NIC Analysis®—what consequences set up the actions taken and so on. The explosion of the Deepwater Horizon oil drilling platform in the Gulf of Mexico led to many published case studies that went back in time to look at the chain of related actions and intended and unintended consequences that began with the decision to drill in that area. The learning that comes from such analyses is only as good as the changes in assessing and managing new behaviors going forward.

Teaching Values

Children learn how to behave and how to name values through the consequences they receive. If schools and parents and others more often recognize the positive social values demonstrated by children such as waiting in line, sharing a toy, giving a cookie to a friend, thanking another, and taking turns on the swing, the children begin to identify those values as socially important. The young students described earlier that we observed did just that when given the opportunity.

Our neighbor told a story about how a well-intended teacher told her second grade students that how they acted mattered and she wanted them to demonstrate good behavior, that is, values-based behavior. She posted a good behavior and a bad behavior list on the bulletin board, which students helped her create. Students' names were posted every day next to their particular list. Those who made the good list demonstrated exceptional skill in the eyes of the teacher in following directions, sitting properly, responding to questions, completing projects on time, raising hands, doing what was asked in an orderly and polite manner, and showing respect to the teacher—all patterns she valued.

Our friend's daughter, Amy, finally made the good list and she was very proud that she made it for "showing respect in how I asked for extra paper." Her father, our neighbor, was impressed that Amy knew why she made the list. It indicated to him that the teacher kept behavior in mind while attaching a higher social good to it (asking in a manner that showed respect), and that this teacher was aware that children needed to understand how their behavior impacts a social contract. Then Amy said, "Daddy, Jamie made the bad list today. He told me it was a better list than the good list." He asked her how you make the bad list. Amy said, in all seriousness, "You have to be a boy to make that list." Behaviors that got your name on the bad list were those such as talking out loud during quiet time, interrupting, and laughing at others' mistakes. The teacher as well as students easily identified those as disrespectful.

The teacher made a mistake that is all too easy to make when trying to teach values. She assumed that the words *good* and *bad* would be sufficient labels to keep students off of the bad list and that their *character* would keep them from wanting to do those wrong behaviors. However, the boys were positively reinforced by the conditions and people surrounding them when they made the bad list. When placed on the list, each person may have felt embarrassed (perhaps), but other students laughed and smiled at them, most likely thumbs up occasionally if the teacher was not looking and, when on the playground, other students encouraged them to describe what they did to make the list. The behaviors that got them on the bad list were clearly not ones parents would want their children to find reinforcing.

Of course these second grade boys were more like the cousins in the Cousin Bill story. They reinforced each other with great glee for behaviors that became highly reinforcing, and they learned how to model the behavior to get their name put up on the list. This well-intended teacher had quickly fallen into a trap of reinforcing the demonstration of the very behaviors she was seeking to eliminate. To reinforce and build good behaviors, she needed to be much more alert to the effects of consequences on behavior.

The teacher's attention on deviant or off-target behaviors by posting names and most likely expressing disapproval or requests for the student to show good manners, etc., became badges of honor, becoming by themselves reinforcing. Clearly, her disapproval was not as reinforcing to the boys as the social reinforcers that came from being on the bad list. It did not mean that they did not like her or appreciate what she was asking of them. She was kind, well-intended, and considered a good teacher. Nevertheless, the bad list boys got a lot more positive, immediate, and certain reinforcers from peers. Nothing really bad happened in making the list except for the teacher's expressed disappointment and perhaps a little shock and awe, which of course was most likely a PIC to the boys.

A most important point of this story is that making the list tells us nothing about the personal moral character of these boys. It does not tell us whether or not these boys held fundamentally "bad values" or if they wanted to disrespect the teacher or harm their fellow students. It only tells us that there were many positive, immediate, and certain reinforcers for doing and saying things that got them added to the list. If you want to promote good behavior in a group setting, explore the *Good Behavior Game* (GBG[26]), an excellent evidence-based model for strengthening appropriate academic and social skills and reflecting stated values.

The behaviors we want to promote in our culture may need to be more often clearly defined, pinpointed, and reinforced in our own behavior patterns and in those of others. The values we attach to such behavior can be more easily recognized by children (and adults) when we attach words to it, as in, "When you gave half of your cookie to your friend, Masako, you showed me that you are a kind and helpful friend." When you as a team member told Francisco that his leading the meeting without interrupting and interpreting others as they provided ideas (something he did all the time), demonstrated that he really meant it when he said he wanted team members to speak up and that he wanted to hear their input. More behavior change may be needed to get a real match for Francisco's expressed value of wanting to hear from his team and what he does afterwards, but this is a good start.

How our behavior impacts others is a large part of living a values-driven life—speaking out loud what we want to do from a values perspective is equally important—and finally actually doing what we say we are going to do. Ask yourself how some of your actions, including your words, do or do not demonstrate core values. Do you identify the effect you want to achieve? If you see things missing, consider how you can begin to demonstrate more of what is needed. Starting with ourselves is always a good place to begin.

Balancing Values in a Pluralistic Society

Many religious and spiritual sources are available to help define how to live a values-driven life. Many of these references begin with religion. In a society such as ours, there are those who do not believe in a religion or, as believers, may see values differently based on the religious creed they espouse. Rarely are there absolutes that you can say, "Do these things and you will always live a life of ethical and values-based behavior." Even *do unto others*, the Golden Rule, has its own problems because at times you may do to others what you value for yourself and that may be very wrong for someone else. Intention to do the right thing is important, but effects are where the rubber meets the road.

In a complex and pluralistic society, it can help to establish a values-based scorecard by which to balance a variety of choices, in striving to be ethical. Use this scorecard to measure how well you are doing in promoting and living a life that includes a definition of the rights of the individual, common good, fairness to those in need, and your effects on others. Such a scorecard will not tell you if you made the right choices but it will tell you if you have considered essential elements in deciding what to do.

While there are many things to consider, the following decision-making criteria can help you evaluate the wisdom in the choices you make when selecting one pattern of behavior over another in a given situation.

- Does it promote the common good?
- Does it convey respect for the individual and/or the group?
- Does it include the concept of fairness (the rights of all) as well as equity (the needs of the less powerful)?
- Does it include your own self-interests?

You may find that one of these values is of greater significance than another, and at other times, two or more are of equal importance (Lattal and Clark, 2007).[27]

Live a Better Life

While simple in terms of description, the science of behavior is complex, dealing with every facet of what we say and do. Developing a greater sense of values-based decision-making requires pinpointing the behaviors you need and to associate doing those behaviors with the values you believe are important to the larger culture as well as to yourself. Help others do the same. Use new words to describe the aggressive and bossy individual who, for the first time, begins to include his team in a discussion. Take that step of telling the person that not only do you like certain actions he is taking, but those actions demonstrate respectful patterns of behavior toward others. Tell him how he supports core values by such actions. Describe the specific behaviors you see that demonstrate teamwork and caring for the needs of others when you see him doing something that reflects a value you want to reinforce.

Many people are never told directly how their actions create bad teamwork or demonstrate disrespect for others, and they do not necessarily know the specific behaviors that define bad teamwork or disrespect. Many people simply do not think of behavior as the way they can make important values visible through specific actions over time. You can be most helpful by coaching a person along these lines, not just describing the behavior at hand but also by defining the larger social meaning.

That coaching includes children. Giving them words that describe their actions as not only the right ones to do in specific situations but ones that show how they might affect the future—better teams, greater concern for others, showing respect for the rights of another—all help them see how their actions can shape that future world in their everyday actions.

What is known about learning new patterns of behavior is of significance in terms of your happiness and well-being. It can change the destiny of your life and that of those you love. It can ignite the greatest of passions and generate creativity beyond your wildest imagination. It can make work a place of discovery.

The act of learning is a passionate act, even if it occurs in the most unassuming ways: riding a bike, tying a shoelace, flying a kite, solving a math problem, or singing a song. All involve the same principles of learning. The principles of learning are also involved in running a school system that excites and enthuses its students; participating in a company that delivers products on time and builds lasting customer relationships; and behaving in ways that keep everyone safe when drilling deep underground or piloting a plane.

This book was written to introduce the science of behavior and to provide pragmatic tools to use in determining what needs to change. It was written so that readers might look at how they show up and how the larger environment supports or impedes them in doing their best. The ease with which biases and stereotypes are formed can be changed as behavior is observed objectivity, and actions of others, whether liked or not, are understood as logical based on their behavioral history.

Becoming objective and moving away from simple labels is the beginning of seeing the potential in others clearly.

Reducing threat and fear to motivate behavior change is something we the authors know is central if learning is to accelerate to high and steady rates. Striving to eliminate punishment, that old trick of nature, as a method we use in dealing with children, our spouse, our neighbors or colleagues, is essential to creating a better world in our everyday lives as well as society as a whole.

Addressing the larger issues of society requires each of us, every day, to decide what values we will strive to demonstrate in our words and actions. To do that well, as this book points out, we need to arrange the conditions that surround us (the full range of PICs and NICs) so that we are likely to do what we say we want to do.

At various times throughout this book, we have mentioned problems of civilization that have thwarted efforts to create a better world: crime, war, pollution, scarcity, pestilence, poverty, and unexpected acts of terror, to name a few. These are problems of human behavior, and our interaction with the broader environment is in need of urgent attention. These behavior-based principles can have specific effects on individuals and large effects on varied cultures. They can also reinforce new ways to engage cooperatively and teach us how to interact with one another, without the use of coercion or aggression for getting our way. But it is not easy.

When we reduce the use of labels and stereotypes to look at behavior objectively, we are provided a new way to understand varied approaches to living life that are different than our own. Applied correctly, these well-grounded and optimistic principles about the human condition can help us all make wiser and more respectful choices that make the world a better place in which to live.

Endnotes

Introduction

1. Ioannidis, J. (2005). "Why Most Published Research Findings Are False," *PLoS Med.*

Chapter 1

2. PIC/NICAnalysis®: Aubrey Daniels International (ADI) introduced the tool in the early 1980s to help people organize their approach to addressing behavior problems, primarily in business at that time. However, the managers and supervisors quickly applied it to their family and personal lives as well as business issues.

3. Eisenberger, R., Stinglhamber, F. (2011). *Perceived Organizational Support: Fostering Enthusiastic and Productive Employees*. American Psychological Association Books: Washington DC.

Chapter 2

4. Mischel, W. (2014). *The Marshmallow Test*, Hachette Book Group: New York, New York.

Chapter 3

5. Ayllon, Teodoro, & Azrin, Nathan. (1968). *The Token Economy: A Motivational System for Therapy and Rehabilitation*. Appleton Century Crofts: New York.

6. Wooldridge, M. (2013). "Mandela Death: How He Survived 27 Years in Prison," BBC News.
7. Layng, T.V. (2009). "The Search for an Effective Clinical Behavior Analysis: The Nonlinear Thinking of Israel Goldiamond," *The Behavior Analyst.*
8. Mechner, F. (1966). Behavioral Technology and Social Change," Proceedings of the American Management Association. New York: American Management Association.

Chapter 4

9. Ayllon T, Azrin N.H. (1964). "Reinforcement and Instructions with Mental Patients," *Journal of the Experimental Analysis of Behavior.*
10. Acker, L. (1990). "Sidney Slug: A Computer Simulation for Teaching Shaping Without an Animal Laboratory," *Teaching of Psychology.*
11. Daniels, A. (2009). *Oops! 13 Management Practices that Waste Time & Money*, Performance Management Publications: Atlanta, Georgia.
12. Lovaas, I (1966). *Reinforcement Therapy*, Smith, Kline and French Laboratories.

Chapter 5

13. Lindsley, O. R. (1992). "Precision Teaching: Discoveries and Effects," *Journal of Applied Behavior Analysis.*

Chapter 7

14. Colvin, G. (2008). *Talent is Overrated*, Penguin Group: New York, New York.
15. Gilbert, T. (2013). *Human Competence: Engineering Worthy Performance*, Pfeiffer: New York, New York.
16. Snyder, G. (2013). "Morningside Academy: A Learning Guarantee, *Performance Management Magazine.*

Chapter 8

17. Michael, J. (1982). "Distinguishing between discriminative and motivational functions of stimuli." *Journal of the Experimental Analysis of Behavior, 37*, 149–155; Michael, J. (1993). "Establishing operations." *The Behavior Analyst, 16*, 191–206.

18. Sidman M. (1966). *Operant Behavior: Areas of Research and Application*, Appleton-Century-Crofts: New York, New York.

19. Schneider, S. (2012). *The Science of Consequences,* Prometheus Books: Amherst, New York.

Chapter 9

20. Than, K. (2015). "What is Darwin's Theory of Evolution?" *Live Science.*

21. Sidman, M. (2000). *Coercion and Its Fallout*, Berrett-Koehler Authors Cooperative: Oakland, California.

22. Tucci, V. (2015). Learning Solutions, Inc. *www.tuccionline.com.*

23. Eisenberger, R., Stinglhamber, F. (2011). *Perceived Organizational Support: Fostering Enthusiastic and Productive Employees.* American Psychological Association Books: Washington DC.

Chapter 10

24. Snopes.com. (2015). *www.snopes.com.*

25. Association of Behavior Analysis International (ABAI). (2015). *https://www.abainternational.org/.*

Chapter 11

26. https://www.air.org/topic/education/good-behavior-game.

27. Lattal, A., Clark R. (2007). *Good Day's Work: Sustaining Ethical Behavior and Business Success.* McGraw Hill: New York, New York.

About the Authors

 **Aubrey C. Daniels, Ph.D**., a thought leader and internationally recognized expert on management, leadership, safety and workplace issues, is considered an authority on human behavior in the workplace. As founder and chairman of the board of directors of his consulting firm, Aubrey Daniels International, he and his staff help organizations employ the timeless principles of behavioral science to re-energize the workplace, optimize performance and achieve lasting results. Aubrey actively blogs about performance systems, workplace safety and management issues, and is frequently interviewed by major media outlets.

In addition to being a highly sought-after keynote speaker at major association, conference and educational events, Aubrey is the author of six best-selling books widely recognized as international management classics: *Bringing out the Best in People: How to Apply the Astonishing Power of Positive Reinforcement*; *Performance Management: Changing Behavior That Drives Organizational Effectiveness*, *Other People's Habits*, *Measure of a Leader*, *Oops! 13 Management Practices that Waste Time and Money (and what to do instead)*, and *Safe by Accident?* His books have been translated into Japanese, Chinese, Korean, Spanish and French and have been licensed in China, India, Indonesia, Japan, Korea, Romania and Saudi Arabia.

A. Darnell Lattal, Ph.D.,

has spent her career working to increase understanding of how the conditions that surround behavior accelerates individual and group accomplishments while reducing the use of threat and fear to control behavior, whether addressing child abuse or misaligned cultures of the workplace.

Darnell attended the University of Alabama (B.A., American Studies, English majors; Sociology-Economics, minors, 1965; M.A. Special Education, 1968), Johns Hopkins University (Honors; advanced studies in education/multicultural studies, 1970), and West Virginia University (Ph.D. in clinical psychology; 1980). She was licensed as a clinical psychologist in 1982 after an internship in oncology and pain management.

Dr. Lattal co-authored *Workplace Ethics: Winning the Integrity Revolution* (Rowman & Littlefield, 1993; University Press, 1998); *Ethics at Work* (Performance Management Publications, 2005); *A Good Day's Work* (McGraw Hill, 2008); and *Sustaining a Stress Free Workplace Using Positive Reinforcement* (English title translation) (Toyo Keiza Press 2010). She has published in refereed journals and the popular press, continuing to write and present at conferences and in webinars. She worked in special education, clinical settings, medical facilities, and university administration before joining a series of Organizational Behavior Management companies. In 1997 she joined Aubrey Daniels International and later became its CEO and President. After retiring in 2014, she served as the Executive Director of the Aubrey Daniels Institute, a 501c3. Currently, she serves the Cambridge Center for Behavioral Studies as a member of the Board of Directors, the Board of Advisors for the University of Alabama's College of Arts & Sciences, and as a founding board member of Women@theFrontier, a non-profit dedicated to furthering women's opportunities through role modeling, education, and mentor development across the world. Her current interests are in supporting research on cooperation and conflict reduction using behavioral strategies.

Her life is made complete by her husband Andy, their three children and loving spouses, and seven delightful grandchildren to whom this book is dedicated.

Additional Resources

 Performance Management
Aubrey C. Daniels
Jon S. Bailey

 Other People's Habits
Aubrey C. Daniels

 *Measure of a Leader*
Aubrey C. Daniels
James E. Daniels

 *Bringing Out the Best in People*
Aubrey C. Daniels

 A Good Day's Work
Alice Darnell Lattal
Ralph W. Clark

 *Safe By Accident*
Aubrey C. Daniels
Judy Agnew

 Head Strong
Ted Ayllon

 *Behaving Well*
Edmund Fantino

Visit our online store at www.aubreydaniels.com/store

About Aubrey Daniels International

Founded in 1978, and headquartered in Atlanta, GA, Aubrey Daniels International (ADI) provides clients with the tools and methodologies to help move people towards positive, results-driven accomplishments and improve their business:

- **Assessments:** scientific analyses of the impact of systems, processes, structures, and practices
- **Executive Coaching:** helping executives apply a behavioral lens to improve their impact on others and the organization
- **Coaching for Rapid Change®:** *a systematic process for focusing managers and leaders to shape positive actions*
- **Surveys:** *a complete suite of proprietary surveys*
- **Certification:** *ADI-endorsed mastery of client skills in our key products, processes, and/or technology*
- **Seminars & Webinars:** *a variety of engaging programs*
- **Scorecards & Incentive Pay**: *an alternative to traditional incentive pay systems*
- **Safety Solutions**: *surveys, assessments, behavior-based safety, and safety leadership training and coaching*
- **Expert Consulting:** *specialized, hands-on direction and support*
- **Speakers**: *accredited and celebrated thought leaders*
- **Blitz Precision Learning®:** web-based application for developing, delivering, and administering training lessons